AF472394

Across my World

An Anthology of Poetry and Life

by

Graham Woodall

and friends

Copyright © 2007 Graham Woodall

The right of Graham Woodall to be identified as author of this work has been asserted by him in accordance with the Copyright, Designs and Patents Act 1988

All rights reserved.
No part of this publication may be reproduced, stored in a retrieval system, or transmitted, in any form or by any means, without the prior permission in writing of the publisher, nor be otherwise circulated in any form of binding or cover other than that in which it is published and without a similar condition including this condition being imposed on the subsequent purchaser

First Edition 2007 (September)
Revised 2007 (October)
Second revision 2007 (November)

ISBN: 978-0-9556771-0-6

www.lulu.com

PREFACE

'Summer of Love' was not the first of my poems but it was the first that could lay any claim at all to being a serious poem and it is certainly the earliest example of my work that has survived the passage of time. There are those who might argue that it is not a poem at all; for what it is worth, I regard it as free verse. Whatever it is, its fortieth birthday in 2007 is sufficient excuse for me to publish this anthology.

But more of that later. In the ranking list of un-revised old poems, my great grandfather, Walter Woodall, occupies the first two places although it is theoretically possible that the first of those should go to his son, my great uncle, also Walter, who might actually have been the very advanced five year old that the poem implicitly credits him with being! He certainly had a very talented poetess as a grand-daughter many years later so perhaps she received some of her inspiration from him, or maybe it's all in the genes. She is Tina Negus I am very happy to include some of the work of both her and another member of my bloodline, Brian Woodall as well as examples of the intuitive poetry of my wife, Denise, and that of my dear friends, John and Jean Bacon.

The poems in "The Sisi Set' are in a class of their own. In a way, they pre-date the work of both Walters but, in another way, they are of very recent vintage. Poems written in the second half of the nineteenth century, to conventional rhyming patterns and metres, but in German and on subjects relevant to the Austrian Empire in general and to its Empress in particular, have previously been translated by others into English on a literal word for word basis. I took those poems and re-translated them using a great deal of licence to restore their original poetic forms as closely as possible and, whilst retaining a certain amount of the original meanings, I have made some attempt at bridging the years by giving the words a relevance to the present century, and not just from an Austrian viewpoint.

At some point in time, soon after the dawn of the Third Millennium, my life-long affection for poetry underwent something of a renaissance which coincided with the realisation that but a handful of those men who fought in the 1914-1918 war remained alive. The inevitable compound formed by the fusion of those two elements was war poetry. As with so many others before me, the 'war' in 'war poetry' primarily means for me the 1914-1918 conflict.

With the exception of the Zulu war poem 'Isandlwana', my own war poetry is entirely based on or around that debacle, that embarrassment of history, that disgraceful episode in the evolution of mankind from a species that only killed for food, and never its own kind, to a species that learned nothing from 'the war to end all wars'. It was only an episode, perhaps, but one that has inspired, and still continues to inspire, more poetry than any other, before or since.

But this book is about more than First World War poetry. In fact it is about more than poetry. It is about life and about part of my journey through life. It is about some of those I have met on the way and about others that I wish I had met. I have arranged the poems into categories that form convenient chapters rather than attempt to place them in any chronological order, either according to when they were written or according to the respective dates of the subject matter. Some poems would have fitted equally well in to different chapters and some should perhaps have been omitted completely but this is a 'warts and all' work.

The narrative parts are not an academic analysis of the poetry. Even if I had wished them to be that, I would have failed for want of the appropriate training: I am anything but an academic! The reader can look for the rhymes, half-rhymes and para-rhymes, and for the iambi, the allusions, the alliterations and the onomatopoeiae - they are all in there. Rather, they combine to make a comment on the reasons why respective poems were written and why they were written in the forms that they were. To this extent it is inevitable that some comment is made on the structure of the poems, but only with 'Isandlwana' do I lay claim to any originality of form.

It is nevertheless necessary to include some pointers to the meaning of certain poems which might otherwise be misunderstood, although I have paid some heed to the school of thought that once a poem is written it becomes as much the property of the reader as it was the writer and both may therefore attribute their own meaning to it. I can only offer my own and leave the reader to decide the extent to which I have been faithful to Wilfred Owen's belief that the poet must be truthful: beware, I may have lied! I am grateful to all my friends who have helped either by way of contribution, by foreign language advice or by simple encouragement.

Graham Woodall. Lichfield. 2007

CONTENTS:

Places:

Family:

War:

The Sisi Set:

'2020 Vision' is, perhaps, a contrived title based upon a well known expression indicative of good eyesight. However, it suits the piece in two ways and may convey some idea of how I expect the World to look by the end of the second decade of the 21st Century.

Orwell's '1984' was regarded by many as his vision of the World in that year. In truth it was his interpretation of what the world looked like at the time of writing. This was 1948, but to avoid political controversy so soon after the Second World War had fragmented into a series of more local conflicts, he simply changed the order of the last two digits and, by doing so, came to sound like a prophet

Perhaps then, '2020 Vision' is how I see the World already.

The Fourth World is a place inhabited by has-been nations; former leaders such as England having been replaced in prime position from the end of the 19th century by the New World led by the USA.

Third World nations are taking their turn on the ascendancy and ancient civilisations such as China and India, without thus far resorting to conventional war, are poised to take the benefits and comforts that had yet to be discovered or invented when they were leaders of a civilised world before the rise of the European nations.

For a decade to date, England has been led by those who see themselves as World Statesmen eager to stake their place in history on an international stage at the expense of those at home. Far better for them to be seen helping America to blast Iraq into oblivion than at home looking after the interests of the innocent souls who elected them into office and who now have to pay for the bombs

Along with education and other essentials, the National Health Service of which we in Britain were once so proud has, despite the huge sums of hard earned public money being thrown at it, been allowed to wither to the point where it seems that only private health care can be relied upon.

This has to be paid for by the individual who has also contributed to the NHS kitty out of already taxed earnings.

2020 Vision

So now the English enter the Fourth World:
the New one rules for now but, soon, the Third.
Around the globe the Jack was once unfurled
by subjects of the Crown, as free as birds.
Now ancient countries rise again to match
emerging nations on the great ascent
that leads to domination of the patch
once ruled by Europeans, heaven sent.

The sun has set on empires that were proud
to exploit others in their quest for wealth.
Its light now shines for those who shout out loud
but take the power less by force than stealth.
Yet still our leaders seek to please the crowd,
with foreign aid whilst we pay twice for health.

One evening in the early part of 2006 I sat down with a glass of wine, Wolf Blass Yellow Label Cabernet Sauvignon if you must know, to watch the 10 'o' clock news on BBC. The lead item, untypically as I care little about many of the items that news editors seem to think matter, was of interest to me as it reported the death of John Profumo.

Mr. Profumo was a politician of the highest order who fell from grace in 1963 for doing nothing worse than lying to the House of Commons. The same rule applied to everyone would empty about 500 seats these days but his indiscretion had national security implications at the height of the Cold War so he had to go. The matter involved the death of a socialite osteopath, the fall of the Conservative Government to enable the disastrous Wilson era to begin and made household names of a couple of young ladies of dubious morals. The ubiquitous Lord Denning also played a part. Books were written and films made. Throughout the scandal, Profumo's wife, herself a former film star, remained loyal to him and although his political career was over for ever he continued, with her support, in various charitable works right up to his death.

To some extent, the Establishment appeared to forgive him eventually. Others such as Paddy Ashdown and John Major at home, and Bill Clinton on the international stage have shown that the general public sometimes prefers a politician with a touch of sparkle to a squeaky-clean grey figure.

The time was also of enormous personal significance to me. I was entering the grown-up world of secondary school education and, like millions of my contemporaries, becoming increasingly fond of a quartet of young musicians from Liverpool who themselves were to change the World forever over the following few years.

I have a photograph taken by my grandfather, Harold Woodall, whilst we were on holiday in Margate, showing me outside a hotel in which some of the Great Train Robbers were in hiding. They were arrested a few days later and a similar photograph, but without me on it, appeared in the national press. The year ended with the assassination of President Kennedy.

The sonnet 'Dear John' sums up 1963 as I recall it.

Dear John,

Commencing at Cliveden, home of Astor,
a lovely young girl was taken upon
the ride that led to major disaster
for Britain, Stephen and maybe you, John.
A Russian and you were rivals in fun
but the Bay of Pigs was still in the news.
Lies you told, later copied by Clinton
and Valerie showed that Hobson <u>can</u> choose.
Mandy Rice Davies and Denning the Law
joined with the cast on this memorable stage.
Buster and Biggs and the Fabulous Four
with Kennedy's death then took the front page.
Now you have gone in the physical sense
you will be remembered, fifty years hence.

Graham.

It was in the late Summer of 2001 that I decided to register with the 'dot com' phenomenon that was 'Friends Reunited'. My niece, Clare Hanson, had mentioned it to me few weeks earlier but I had never found the spare time to check it out. Then my life-long friend, Ian Fellows, gave me a demonstration of it on his lap-top computer after lunch one Sunday and I was hooked. I joined in the very next day.

For my part this led to the resumption of many friendships that had started at West Bromwich Grammar School almost 40 years earlier and to the forging of many new friendships with non-contemporaries from the same school.

These friendships were corollaries of a huge reunion that a few of us, including Ian, organised in July 2002 to mark the Centenary of the founding of that school In the cases of some of those attending, romantic relationships rather than simple friendships were either renewed or brought to belated fruition. I understand that such developments were repeated in connection with schools from up and down the country and indeed world-wide. Sometimes, marriages were ruined and families broken up for the want of satisfying a twenty year or much longer lasting crush on a former class-mate.

Not having trodden fresh romantic ground myself for many a long year, I wondered how sweethearts from the dim and distant past went about repeating or re-enacting the courtship rituals that we all did as second nature in our youth. The thought of Spring love in the Autumn of life intrigued me and led to the writing of 'Equinox'.

The working title was actually 'Which Equinox?' to reflect my initial assumption that these dear old souls were, in reality, deluded as to which end of their metaphoric lifespan of a year they were nearer to. As the poem evolved, however, a clearer picture emerged for me and proved the old adage correct; you are only as old as you feel!

But remember! Do I always write the truth?

Equinox

Can love lie sleeping, unfulfilled
for forty years or more
and then awake like Spring soil, tilled,
more fruitful than before?

Can hearts combine to beat as one
when weakened by life's tasks?
The passion of young life not gone,
the wrinkles only masks.

Can limbs entwine, that never did,
those urges now to meet
or, as before, must thoughts be hid
within those dreams, so sweet?

Can life be short, as so it seems
as shadows lengthen now,
or is there more beyond those beams
when from this stage we bow?

The answers rest with you my friend
and you and you and you.
For all us lovers know our end
and chances are but few.

I was fortunate enough, in those bomb-site scarred, half-rationed days of austerity that followed World War Two, to be born in the town of West Bromwich in the heart of England. As a direct result of this, as inevitably that night will follow day, I became a follower of West Bromwich Albion Football Club. It was a very successful club in those days, and had already been such for about 80 years, playing at the same home ground since 1900. The glory days continued intermittently until about 1985 when serious decline set in and this decline has still to be fully reversed.

In one of the best periods in history for the Club, a young player from Chester-le-Street, in the North East of England, Bryan Robson, started his career with the Club. He married a local girl who happened to be of my acquaintance, and adopted both town and club as second homes, possibly third homes if you include Manchester, where he was taken when Ron Atkinson became manager of one of the clubs there. Bryan achieved massive success as a player and became an England Captain of great renown,

In 2004 Bryan became Manager of West Bromwich Albion F.C who were struggling to hold on to the place in the top division of English football that they had gained the season before. Whilst some die-hards in the crowd had never forgiven Bryan for leaving the Club years earlier, he was generally regarded as the right man for the job and a wave of optimism for the future of the Club was sustained when relegation was avoided that season. Bottom of the division at the halfway stage, they performed what came to be called 'The Great Escape'. However, this was only temporary and the following season saw re-entry into the lower division. Soon after the start of the 2006/07 season he was asked to leave. This necessitated a revision to 'The Hawthorns', which was originally written to mark his appointment, with the following prophetic last four lines...

'Now Bryan's back, a hero with Great Ron,
whose football talents we can see no more.
For on the field he stood above the rest
but on the line he's yet to stand the test.'

The Hawthorns

The hallowed turf, where mighty men have trod,
is called The Hawthorns or, by some, The Shrine.
And battles have been staged upon this sod
on many days since eighteen ninety nine.

Pennington, Bassett, Bomber and The King
were all great heroes in their time but, since
those glory years, with Willy on the wing,
the faithful few would settle for a prince.

Pretenders to the throne have been and gone
but none has matched the heady heights of yore.
When Bryan came, we thought he was the one
but now his tactics we shall see no more.

For on the field he stood above the rest
but on the line he didn't stand the test

As you may read later, I once spent a holiday in the Austrian region of Salzkammergut, in awe of the lakes and mountains. Soon after returning to England I recalled that it had been many years since I had visited our own Lake District and so Denise and I booked into a hotel in Grasmere for a short stay. I quickly recalled why we had been to the trouble and expense of the journey to Austria as, by comparison to Wolfgangsee and its neighbours, Windemere is now an over-commercialised boating pond with even its swans trained to tamely take tourists' feed, and the hills around it comprise little more than rising shores. Grasmere remains largely unspoilt and whilst both its waters and hills are beautiful and evocative of tranquil stability, the inspiration for poetry that I was expecting to overwhelm me with ideas never quite materialised. This expectation was of course based upon the reputations of William Wordsworth, Samuel T Coleridge and the like; poets from the romantic period forever associated with that region. In truth, I knew little of their work beyond 'I wandered lonely as a cloud', a poem that was more or less compulsory learning for school children of my era. I assumed that in the late 18th and early 19th century not only was the area more stunningly beautiful than it is now in absolute terms but also that the likes of Wordsworth would have lacked the experience of having seen bigger and better versions in Italy, Austria and elsewhere. I can travel, door to door, from my home in Staffordshire to a hotel in Salzburg in a single morning but Wordsworth had no such advantages. He must, I thought, have been so taken by these English lakes and hills that they provided him with sufficient inspiration and interest to fuel a very long lifetime of writing poetry. How wrong I was!!

Inspiration did come after a day or two but in a sadly negative way: I found myself writing a poem that set out to bring Wordsworth down from the pedestal upon which he had been set a century or more before my birth. It was abandoned after the first few lines that went something like this...........

Wordsworth was a one-trick pony
'Daffodils' and not much more.
Even those words were on loan, he
took them from his sister, Dor.
His 'Prelude' was a tiresome story,
far too long and just a bore.

I visited Dove Cottage where he lived for many years and which is now part of a museum complex with a bookshop. I always find it physically impossible to enter any bookshop and leave empty-handed. I therefore became equipped with a couple of anthologies of Wordsworth's work, together with a biography. I found that he had written over 400 sonnets, a favourite poetic form of mine too, and volume after volume of other work. I cannot say that I was converted to being a Wordsworth devotee, as I would not describe more than about one fifth of the total as being to my taste. However, it did become clear to me that he was not the parochial bumkin that I had taken him to be, by a country mile! He did live a long life, dying soon after his 80th birthday, and he did spend a great deal of it in the English Lake District. However, what I had not previously realised was that, in his younger days, he and a friend had WALKED about 3000 miles in 12 weeks to see, amongst other sights, the Alps, the Saint Gothard Pass and the Italian lakes. With the same friend he also spent a great deal of time in the Snowdon area of Wales, taking in more splendid views, and he was therefore at least as well informed as a post World War II baby-boomer like me, and all without my advantages of jet powered aeroplanes and high speed trains.

It wasn't all sight-seeing either. For a start, the said friend, a Robert Jones, had no less than three single and available sisters at home whilst Wordsworth was staying in Wales! During his 'Grand Tour' he had developed a relationship with a French girl, Annette Vallon, which had resulted in the birth of his first child, Caroline, in late 1792. To add to the romance of it all, England and France went to war in February 1793 thus preventing him from returning to France for many years or, perhaps, giving him the perfect excuse not to! One can only speculate as to the goings-on at Dove Cottage, which appears to have been transformed at times into an opium den by Coleridge.

Against this background and his years at Cambridge University, he could not be regarded by any means as being unworldly and I considered that it behove me to cease work immediately on the untitled poem I had begun and to write something much more respectful. I decided to convert him to a First World War poet travelling again, this time as a ghost, through Europe in 1918 or thereabouts. The result was "The Spirit of Wordsworth' and any similarity it may have to 'Daffodils' is purely intentional!

The Spirit of Wordsworth

I floated wanly in my shroud,
without the Opium-eater's pills,
and saw the poppies growing proud
like ghosts of dancing daffodils.
A million men brought to their knees
and then to die with rats and fleas.

Those blood-red blooms were not in line
but, scattered, sprang forth from the clay.
Their simple splendour was a sign
that should our fear of death allay.
A sign that life came not by chance,
that loveless landscape to enhance.

As I beheld this bright array,
the blackened branches of a tree
returned me to the fearsome fray
fought, some had said, to make them free.
Did all that crimson come to nought
just like before, when France we fought?

A hundred years had passed since I
bore witness to an earlier feud.
Another score and, from the sky,
the rain of death shall there be viewed.
Is it eternal that Man kills
to save his own, or take his thrills?

I have often found that the inspiration or idea for a poem comes from another, sometimes also written by me as will be seen, but usually from one or more written by others.

'Historic Journey' claims its parentage from both of these sources.

Having written 'The Spirit of Wordsworth', a poem that casts William Wordsworth as a Great War poet, I decided to create a connection between Wordsworth and the man who for me is the greatest of Great War poets, Wilfred Owen.

It is well known that Owen, possibly shell-shocked, possibly concussed from a fall or possibly for some other reason, was sent to Craiglockhart Hydropathic Establishment in Edinburgh for treatment by Dr. Rivers. Here, he became editor of the house journal and, through it, his own first publisher

He also met Siegfried Sassoon there and their friendship was very influential on Owen's work and life, short that it was to be afterwards. Sassoon was at best bisexual and many friends and acquaintances to whom he introduced Owen had even clearer preferences for same-sex relationships. Owen didn't live long enough for conclusions to be reached either way. The sexual orientation of Dr. Rivers is not entirely clear.

Owen travelled North by train to Edinburgh's Waverley Station and, not surprisingly, slept through much of the long journey, passing close to the region of his childhood on the way. It is not a giant leap of the imagination to say that in his dreams he may have stopped off a few miles south of his eventual destination to meet some predecessor poets and to share with them his habitual cigarettes, although possibly enhanced in flavour and effect by Coleridge.

In addition to having the sonnet form favoured by both Wordsworth and Owen, 'Historic Journey' makes deliberately exaggerated use of what Poet Laureate John Masefield once called Owen's 'continuous alliterative assonance'. I can confidently leave the many other allusions in this poem for the reader to find.

Historic Journey

The time when Wilfred went by Windemere,
a wet and windswept weekend whilst unwell,
Craiglockhart was the place to clear the mire
that wound his wits into a woolly whirl.
His train, Waverley-bound, sent him to sleep
but in his dreams he saw the waters, calm,
and vales of browning leaves beneath the slope
of soaring hillsides he would never climb.

In reverie he met the Grasmere Set,
took poppies with his Gold Flake, as they did
and, with Dove Cottage as his dugout, sat
to wonder who still lived and who was dead.
By Dunbar's shores he woke and smoothed his suit
and went to Rivers, straight in thought and deed.

I have already mentioned the Centenary Reunion of my old school. When the school was founded, in 1902, a language teacher by the name of John Carroll joined the Staff and stayed for 35 years. In 1906 his French wife presented him with a daughter who later attended the same school before taking a degree at Birmingham University and subsequently becoming a major film star with over forty leading parts to her credit in films ranging from 'The Guns of Loos' to Hitchcock's 'The Thirty Nine Steps'.

She was Madeline Carroll and she was at one time described as being the most beautiful woman in the World.

Her nationality remains the subject of some debate, varying between that of her father, that of her mother, that of her birth, that of her various husbands and that of her various residences. Probably for that reason, she was never officially honoured by Britain, as would certainly be expected by a star of half her magnitude today, for no reason other than for being famous. This was despite the fact that she effectively foreshortened her glittering career in favour of charitable work during World War II.

Old Throstles, as former pupils of the said school are known, have tried in some way to give her the recognition we think she deserves and to supplement similar aspirations by a local historian, Terry Price, an admirer who has been successful in placing a monument and various commemorative plaques in her honour in the town of her birth. Her graduation from Birmingham University in 1926 was commemorated on the Roll of Honour of the old school and remains to this day.

Although her life overlapped mine by about 35 years, we never met but I have had the honour and pleasure to have met her cousin, Ciaran O'Carroll who takes an interest in both the town and the school where his Uncle Jack lived and worked, and in preserving the memory of his cousin.

My own contribution to her centenary year in 2006 was a poem which requires little further explanation other that to mention that although my head has been almost completely hair-free for some years, it was once described by Thomas Turner, another Old Throstle and Chairman of the School Governors when I was a pupil, as 'a field of corn'.

Sonnet to an Old Throstle

Oh Madeleine, why were you there so soon?
At twice my mother's age when I was born
there never was a chance that you might swoon
to see my golden hair – a field of corn!
The guns of Loos fired in my granddad's time,
your film of them came when his son was four.
The Tower opened with you in your prime,
they queued on ev'ry step up to the door.

Old Throstles saw you forming as a bud
that blossomed fully when you crossed the foam.
By then you'd left this land for Hollywood
but further conflict started close to home
so greater fortunes you trod in the mud
as battlefields of Europe you would roam.

'Janus' is another example of one poem inspiring another. In choosing the title for 'Equinox', it occurred to me that, as the word itself signifies the two occasions each year when the day and the night are of equal length, why then does the 'nox' dominate?

I have no idea what the true answer to that question might be although I have little doubt that there is such an answer. It did give me the idea to write about all sorts of situations in which the same basic fact could be viewed in two directly opposite ways, according to the mood or personality of the party involved.

The working title for the poem was 'Equidies' with the intention of balancing up the general and usual over-use of the word 'equinox'. However, thoughts of Janus, the two faced creature of mythology, rose to the surface during the writing stage and so that is what it came to be called.

It starts with the familiar analogy of the glass which appears half-empty to one person and half-full to another.

It then proceeds to raise equivalent questions about a whole raft of situations from daily life, some of which probably never occur outside my own head.

I encourage the feeding of Robins, Blue Tits, Finches, Sparrows and the like in my own garden, even the widely despised Magpie, but yet I have to resist the temptation to take an air rifle to Pigeons. Why should that be?

Is a male-dominated nursery rhyme still sexist when the boy comes a cropper before the girl?

I shall leave the other lines unexplained, the poem is simple enough without me spelling out even the less-obvious meanings.

Janus

Is the glass half empty or half full?
Is to work a curse or a treat?
Does Summer rain refresh or annoy?
Does a draw equate to defeat?

Is fifty five into middle age?
Is three score years and ten enough?
Does it feel warm for the time of year?
Does living a soft life feel tough?

Is the baking Sun the farmer's friend?
Is a rainy July preferred?
Does a 'B' grade make you smile or frown?
Does a pigeon rank as a bird?

Is a long, dark night cosy and snug?
Is a Winter's day far too short?
Does cooking at home become a chore?
Does home-made taste better than bought?

Is sowing or reaping better loved?
Is a hard place better than rocks?
Does Jack beat Jill, falling downhill?
Does Equidies beat Equinox?

As I said in my Preface, 'Summer of Love' has a claim to being the first of my serious poems. It was written in 1967 and, for reasons long since forgotten if ever known, it was originally entitled 'Napoleon Complex'. By the time I revised the work circa 1982, 'the summer of love' was the definitive description of 1967 and also summed up the prevailing mood at the time I wrote the words. Hence the title. It can also lay claim to being the first of a very small number of my poems that was actually commissioned. My close friend and cultural guru, Alan Cartwright, was compiling an anthology to which he was intending to give the rather presumptuous title of 'The Rubber Hat of Omar Cartwright", presumably also intending to give appropriate acknowledgement to Mr Kayam, and was looking for contributions.

In those days I used to spend many hours in Dartmouth Park, West Bromwich, with various friends including Alan. On one such occasion I came upon an old man, probably a tramp but not begging, and I developed an irresistible urge to help him. In my pocket I had a pound note and a two shilling piece. Secure in the knowledge that I would be able to purchase the latest Beatles record, a packet of cigarettes, a couple of pints of beer and still have change from the pound note, I gave the man the coin. The intention was good but my clumsy execution of the gift is not something of which I should be particularly proud. I did no more than toss the money to him with the condescending shout of "Here, Mate, get yourself some dinner".

He could have bought a fish and chips meal, as was my wish, but alternatively he could have bought a pint of beer or ten cigarettes and it did occur to me that both of the last two options would be more likely than the first. He was therefore very much like me whilst remaining very much like the bee I was watching earlier – eagerly taking what he needed from what he found in the park.

My use of the word 'trudging' was not consciously taken from Owen's 'Dulce et Decorum est', it was a word that was frequently used by my mother and by her mother. The phrase 'pound in my pocket' pre-dated Wilson's devaluation speech by several months.

I had no way of knowing it at the time but the image of that man remains with me still and came to the fore many years later when he became the subject of a second poem, 'The Old Soldier'.

Summer of Love

Here I sit on a hot, sultry day
watching a bee buzzing around
on thin, delicate wings.
I see a man, a tired old man
trudging in thin, delicate boots
and carrying a worn out raincoat
out of habit, not need, this fine day.
The pound in my pocket will be spent
on cigarettes and beer and music.
"Baby you're a rich man" sings John
and he's right – he always is.
The florin I fling with kind contempt
will buy food for the man today.
Or will it? I must wonder.
Are we so different, the man, the bee and I?

In the 1960s, a period during which many of the motorways and dual carriageways of Great Britain were designed and constructed, quantity surveyors and land surveyors handling those types of project grew both in number and importance. However, the qualifying and regulatory bodies to which they belonged had been founded in earlier times, times in which such projects were regarded as part of the building industry or had been dealt with by the Military. The term 'civil engineering' is one intended merely to distinguish it from 'military engineering'.

As a consequence, surveyors found that they had to qualify as such by learning skills inappropriate or unrelated to the work they would be doing, or try to build careers without formal qualifications in their specialist field. The situation gave rise to a group of such surveyors forming what became the Institution of Civil Engineering Surveyors of which I became a student member in 1974, qualified in 1979 and went on to be President in 1997.

In 2006 it was announced that the last surviving active member of that founding group was to retire from his post as Executive Director.

He is C. Kevin Blackwell, who was, for many years, as fond of his Florida holiday home as he was of Old Trafford, home of his beloved Manchester United Football Club, whilst remaining faithful to his real home and to the Sale headquarters of the I.C.E.S. There is little doubt that he will remain close to the Institution and to the many friends he has made, of which I am proud to be one, on a social basis for many years to come.

The date of the announcement of his retirement coincided with the bicentenary of another iconic figure in the world of civil engineering about whom there is more later but whose initials are similar, Isambard Kingdom Brunel.

This one is just for you, Kevin, in return for many years of friendship and for the ticket to see the first ever Premiership appearance of my team. It was against yours on August 16th 2002.

Our Kevin

Old Trafford and Florida know his name
but his heart and head are both nearer Sale.
It is hard to sing praise, and not sound lame,
as this man's record makes others look pale.
There to begin with, nay, he WAS the start
of I.C.E.S., home for surveyors galore.
His wit has been felt, like a well aimed dart,
all over the World but, sadly, no more.
At least not as leader, now just our friend:
he will long be with us. There, at the bar!
And nothing will change, it is not the end:
what he has constructed time will not mar.
Two hundred years we had IKB.
For many more yet we'll have CKB.

Throughout the 1970s there was a tendency for British construction workers of all types to seek employment in the Middle East for a few years as a means of earning high wages. Massive building projects funded by Arabian oil were underway and salaries up to four times that paid in the UK were being offered, together with tax-free status and numerous other fringe benefits. I was never interested, although in 1977 I gave serious consideration to a two year contract in Saudi Arabia with the UK company employing me at the time. It was only when I saw an example of the way they dealt with wayward Princesses there that the interest ended. If they can publicly execute a member of their own Royal family there is no way of knowing what they might do to me, I thought, and stayed at home. However, in 1988 the island of Jamaica was badly damaged by Hurricane Gilbert and for some reason I immediately became keen to go and help with the restoration of the buildings. My then employer agreed and I went to work in Kingston with substantial financial benefits and a chance of adventure. The working conditions were hard but the social life was quite good, spoiled only by repeated bouts of digestive difficulties. After a few weeks, my good friend and colleague, Andrew Carleton, joined the team and became my room-mate at the Liguanee Club. For a month we then suffered together and took full advantage of the social scene in the evenings and weekends, Andrew being a natural entertainer and bon viveur. We saw many interesting sights including the prison yard mentioned at the start of Bob Marley's song, 'No woman, no cry' and, in dealing with several matters of hurricane damage suffered by his widow, Rita, we were called to her house on Skyline Drive.

We returned to UK just before Christmas and Andrew did the round of parties entertaining everyone with his hilarious versions of our experiences in the Caribbean, mostly embellished but to great effect. Our friendship had been formed a few years earlier when we were both having certain life problems, mainly shortage of money. However, the Jamaica adventure sealed that friendship which continued to develop into the new millennium.

I wrote 'Carleton came' early in 1989 but more recently revised the third stanza to reflect one aspect of our later life, Karaoke singing. It could have been invented for us and the early signs of that were the taking over the microphone from a professional singer at a cabaret in Ocho Rios one weekend, the episode upon which the original version was based.

Carleton came

I had no wish to work abroad
when chances came to build there.
So why was I so easily made
to think that I must go where
damaged structures had been brought
to ruin by Gilbert's blowing?
To get away? To have a break?
To pay the money owing?

For weeks I toiled beneath the Sun
and spent each evening drinking.
But every hour I had to run
because my guts were sinking.
Then Carleton came and all was well,
my old mate gave me reason
to do my time and stay the course
until the Christmas Season.

Together at The Liguanee
we never did stop joking,
The Queen of Spades, the Vaseline,
the snooker and the soaking.
The days up North, the ganja man,
the karaoke singing
then back to Kingston and Bob's yard
with Rita's Skyline ringing.

In Birmingham he told those tales,
his audience were in stitches.
And tears of laughter wet my cheeks
with joy beyond all riches.
A bond that formed when we were sad
was stronger with us cheerful.
My friend for life, and then beyond,
of that do not be fearful.

From about 1989 onwards my friendship with Andy Carleton grew from that of workmates who enjoyed a lunchtime drink to that of close friends. In our impoverished past I had once given him an overcoat that, by then, I had owned for no less than twenty years, simply because he didn't have one and I had two. Always a man of fashion, Andy would rather shiver than wear it but he did swap it with one his father had and he did, therefore, derive some benefit from my gift.

Twice a year throughout the 1980s, our working colleagues spent an entire Saturday on a coach tour of public houses, alternatively in Dovedale and Shropshire, as young men are wont to do. I had young children at home at that time and always declined offers to join the days out despite Andy regaling me with up-beat accounts of each trip in the pub the following Monday lunchtime. By 1989, I had been converted and joined the trips thereafter, the Shropshire trip always coinciding with the F. A. Cup Final which was watched on TV in the pub at which we took lunch.

Andy's daughter, Ashleigh, was about four years old when I first got to know him and his son, Baillie, was born a year or two later. I became fond of both of them and took enormous pride and pleasure in attending Ashleigh's Wedding Celebrations in 2006. Another daughter, Nicola, was born in 1991 but, temporarily I hope, I have lost touch with her since 2001.

Andy took and passed the examinations of the Chartered Institute of Loss Adjusters and sought my coaching as a Chartered Surveyor when preparing for the paper on Building. He passed it with Distinction and it remained a source of amusement to him that I only achieved a basic pass!

Subversive moves were made by some to create a professional situation that, as a by-product not an objective, could have driven a wedge between Andy and I but they did not succeed in either respect. To my great sadness, Andy died in 2001 after a five year battle against a brain tumour. Our friendship lives on through his family.

He was a great admirer of the musician, Sting, to whom he bore a physical resemblance and, as the song that was played at his funeral suggests, he'll be watching us!

Now he's gone

A poem to his honour I once wrote
when we were all much brighter than today.
We laughed about when I gave him a coat,
he swapped for one of Russ's, by the way.
The Dovedale trips, and those to Clun as well,
I missed for years until I found my way.
On Monday lunchtimes he would always tell
me what they'd done the previous Saturday.

As years passed by, a family bond we made,
his children, two then three, became mine too.
By training, our foundations were well laid,
despite the tricks of others we'd the glue
to hold the friendship that will never fade.
Death has its Sting but, Andy, we have you.

At the age of five I contracted the childhood disease known as measles. Despite closed curtains to limit my exposure to bright light, the illness left me with a weak left eye. I was prescribed spectacles for reading and writing but I was never convinced that they were actually of any use. Horrible things they were, with hook-shaped springs that wrapped around the ears to secure the apparatus against the energetic excesses of youngsters, I presume. Personally, I have never been that energetic whilst either reading or writing so the technology was superfluous in my case.

By the age of fifteen I was being told that I no longer needed to wear the spectacles but by thirty I was finding that my eyes became tired after a few hours' close work and I therefore resumed the practice of wearing spectacles, albeit without the spring loading! This happy situation continued, with a change of equipment every few years and with the lens on the right side being almost plain glass whilst the left increasingly took on the appearance of the bottom of a milk bottle.

But then I turned fifty and my right eye joined the list of anatomical parts that were reaching their 'best by date'. It wasn't a major problem at first but it was nevertheless irritating to have to fumble for aid to read a menu, a railway timetable, a football programme to check the name of the opposition full-back who had just fouled one of our men, or to pick up a message on my cell-phone. I remained able to see action on the far side of the pitch or in the further goal mouth from my seat in the East Stand.

Conversely, I was unable to drive a car or even to walk about the house safely whilst wearing my prescribed reading glasses. I was able to conduct building surveys as well (or as badly) as ever except that, when in poor light indoors, I had to use specs to write down my observations. It was deliberate concealment by the operators, not my poor eyesight, that caused my failure on several occasions to spot speed cameras and thereby find myself compelled to make cash contributions to the Home Office.

The final straw came on 14th February 2006 when the 'chip and pin' system became standard. For years I had been able to scrawl my signature on credit card slips, knowing that anywhere near the bottom would do. With chip and pin you need to be able to see what the machine is telling you to do at any given moment.

Action was clearly required and I therefore consulted my optician who came up with the idea of a varifocal contact lens. My right eye was still just about good enough to work unaided, provided that the very weak left eye could be encouraged to share the job of seeing. So, until I could become accustomed to using these things, I was given a single small disc of soft, transparent plastic to moisten then apply to the surface of my left eye. When I eventually managed to insert the lens I could appreciate the theory of its design but, by then, my eye surround was so sore that the beneficial effect was substantially diminished.

The next two weeks were a continuous battle, first to install the object and then to suffer the discomfort of its presence. The idea of moving onto a pair was abandoned.

Cheap spectacles can be bought at any supermarket or department store and give straightforward magnification. I acquired two matching pairs, one with 1.25X enlargement and the other twice as strong. Using a jewellers' screwdriver, I swapped the lenses to give the stronger lens to my left eye and the weaker one to my right. A great idea but with an adverse effect on my balance and on my judgement of distance, pretty much the same as would a bottle of Courvoisier. Driving would have been both murderous and suicidal.

When the problem first started to develop, my optician suggested bifocal spectacles which I did try at the time but without any success. Now, the time was right and as I walked from Colin Lee's shop in the centre of Lichfield in a pair of very expensive rimless bifocals, I knew that a compromise between the sharp eyes of my youth and the days, still to come, when stronger measures will be required, had been found.

Unfortunately, I now need less light to be able to see and the flip-side of this is that when there is too much light, as I found in the sunshine of Lanzarote on my first bifocal holiday, the dazzle has a negative effect. Conventional sun glasses revert me to 'chip and pin roulette' and my darkened reading glasses make me a menace on the road.

As I write, I have a pair of darkened bifocals on order, watch this space...

Bifocal

I could find a faulty fascia at fifteen feet
and recognise a ridge tile that was wrong.
I could spot a sagging soffit-board from the street
and describe defective down-pipes, badly hung.

I could witness wizard wing-play on the west side
and scintillating saves at Smethwick End.
I could clock a cash-cow camera in its hide,
built to boost Brown's biggest bounty for his friend.

But putting pen to paper, problems to proclaim,
and reading restaurant reckoning, written small,
might mean mistaken memos. Menus? Much the same
when shifting focus from a fractured wall.

A pair of lick-on lenses looked like working well
but foreign bodies bubble in my eyes.
And simple spectacles, the sort that Sainsbury's sell,
would weaken wide-road vision, most unwise!

So what was one to do with eyes they were so weak?
The answer was, as always, very local.
Whilst perfect peeping probably has passed its peak,
without that it is best to be bifocal

When my interest in 'the beautiful game' started, Stanley Matthews was still playing, George Best and Willie Johnston were still at school and David Beckham was two decades away from being born. Jimmy Greaves had yet to make his mark on the game and Jeff Astle, Bobby Moore and Geoff Hurst were completely unknown.

With the enthusiasm and total thoroughness of learning that only youngsters have, I knew all the top players by name (desperate, incidentally, to find one called Graham) but I could not name a single referee. Former referees such as Arthur Ellis and Stanley Rous became well-known but not as referees, the earliest to achieve notoriety (oh, all right then, fame) being a chap called Ken Aston whom I seem to recall being distinguished from the rest simply because he was good at his job. Jack Taylor was a close contemporary and was renowned for similar qualities but, in 1974, he was given the World Cup Final to look after. Having given Holland a first minute penalty, he felt the need to award one to their opponents, West Germany, later in the game. Whether or not either or both were correct decisions is entirely immaterial. The effect was that the spotlight was on the referee at least as much as on the two teams that each contained some of the all time greats of football.

Others then saw the chance to achieve what their lack of football talent would always deny them, that is to say media attention and what they still see as fame and glory. Clive Thomas in effect succeeded Jack Taylor as England's leading referee and some of his decisions were truly astonishing but always kept him in the news. Others yet achieved immortality because of mad decisions, such as Ray Tinkler who allowed my team to score a goal from what every player on the pitch and every supporter in the ground could see was an offside position. This cost Leeds United the game, the league title and a punishment for crowd protest that arguably cost them the title the following season too.

These hangers-on used to be given a medal if they handled the FA Cup Final but now get paid salaries that rival doctors. They dress in all colours as well as black and now need a fourth official as well as two linesmen that they now call assistant referees. All other major sports use modern technology to decide difficult but important matters and the sooner football does the same and puts referees back where they belong the better.

The Men in the Middle

Those men in black, their henchmen likewise clad,
are truly fireproof and beyond control.
'He robbed us' was the classic chant of those
who saw it all and knew the rules by heart.
In better days their nameless, faceless form
was rarely seen except in shades of grey.
They knew their place, were grateful for the chance
to sweep the stage where better men had played.
Their part, the most despised on Saturday,
was more or less forgotten in a week
and, once a year, their breed had its big day;
a medal from the Monarch, not a fee.
The taste of power once caused Leeds to miss
their title aspirations, Thank you Ray.
'I'm bigger than you, Don.' He seemed to say,
the offside rule suspended at his whim.
Then, prior to a Welshman causing strife,
the penny dropped that he was not the first
to write his name as large as greater folk
in whose reflected glory he could bathe.
Not just one but two spot kicks were given
to teams with Beckenbauer and with Cruyff.
No bias shown as He took centre stage
and raised the expectations of his ilk.
For many years they stayed in monochrome
and, by and large, did not proliferate
but then the lure of lucre took effect
and show-off referees became the norm.
Just like the peacocks that they emulate
they now come clad in colours, four at once.
We can but hope that science will succeed
and knock them from the pedestals they've built.

It is fitting at this point to introduce my cousin, Brian Woodall.

Strictly speaking he is my cousin once removed, my father's first cousin, but we can all manage without such trivia; the devil is always in the detail.

Brian may qualify for what I call the 'Neil Kinnock Award' for being the first Woodall in a thousand years to go to university. Certainly he was the first on the direct line of descent that I share with him. Fortunately, as a family, we have progressed to graduate status at least apace with the population as a whole and my own generation boasts about 50% success, with a slightly better score so far for the generation after us, although not all of them have reached university age at the time of writing, and some may not have been conceived yet!

Brian was born in 1935 to my grandfather's youngest brother, Alfred, and his wife, Ethel, and grew up in war-torn Derby. Between then and his graduation from Aberystwyth University in 1958, followed by his teaching certificate from Nottingham University and a teaching career which effectively started at my own old school, he studied at Bemrose School in Derby.

Toward the end of his time at Bemrose, he displayed some poetic tendencies which came to light recently and which he has allowed me to include in this book, sitting alongside the work of several of our shared relatives.

I have not placed his poems in a section of their own and the first one, 'Knocking off time' is about people and so is within that section.

Later you can read 'The Steeple' which is about a place and then 'Autumn' for which I did not have a section (despite having poems that include 'Summer' and 'Spring' in their titles) and so it can be found in the Family section and is therefore categorised according to the identity of its author rather than its subject material.

Knocking-off time

The rain falls dully from a concrete sky,
a barge hoots in the gathering gloom,
pale, drawn faces heave a mutual sigh
as sirens still the droning loom.

A quick surge and a hectic dash for trains,
workers scatter in a seething mass;
crocodiles of cyclists, traffic jams,
the lighted pavements shine like glass.

Brian H. Woodall c.1953

It is perhaps apparent from some of my poems and anecdotes that I am not, by nature, a Socialist. After the death of John Smith, leadership of the Labour Party passed to a youthful Tony Blair. Together with henchmen such as Peter Mandelson and Gordon Brown, he converted the anachronistic remains of his party into an electable entity which came to power in May 1997 and still remains despite having become a busted flush sometime during its second term. Sadly, the Conservative Party has stumbled from one failed leader to another during the same period, searching still for a worthy successor to Margaret Thatcher, and has been unable to put up any worthwhile opposition. In 2007, Blair finally did as he had promised earlier and handed the reins to Gordon Brown. At the height of his potential as one of the great Prime Ministers of all time, which he never did become, he made a big deal of treating education as a priority by his famous 'Education. Education. Education' speech. Unfortunately his ten year sojourn in Downing Street will be remembered for several other things. He soon fell into the trap of believing himself to be omnipotent and developed delusions of adequacy. Filling the void left on the World stage when George W Bush gave up foreign travel after the '9 11' attack, Blair chose to stake his claim for a place in history by declaring war on Iraq, a certain amount of synergy coming from 'Dubya' who, puppet-like, was determined to finish the job his father had started some years before. Blair deceived the British public and Parliament into accepting that Iraq had weapons of mass destruction which could be turned against us in forty five minutes and that this justified the complete disregard of the United Nations. Together they invaded Iraq and remain in occupation of this once-great nation to date. Another hallmark of Blair's reign was the elevation to the Peerage and the award of lesser honours to his buddies, especially the rich ones. Protected as if by a coating of 'Teflon', he escaped all responsibility for those wrongdoings. Part of the art of staying at the top for so long was throwing a scrap to the 'Old Labour' dogs by making John Prescott his Deputy and giving Gordon Brown the job of Chancellor of the Exchequer. With some 'Old Labour' tendencies of his own still lingering, Brown set several time bombs ticking which will explode in the faces of his successors as inflation when the final bills have to be paid. Some shrapnel may strike Brown but Blair will escape completely from this too. Soon after the actual date of his resignation was announced, Blair paid a visit to the Pope. Maybe it was as Head of State rather than as God's man on Earth or maybe it was because he fancies the job himself some day!

Ten Years at Number Ten

Election. Election. Election.
Education. Education. Education.
Delusion. Delusion. Delusion.
Deception. Deception. Deception.
Invasion. Invasion. Invasion.
Occupation. Occupation. Occupation.
Allegation. Allegation. Allegation.
Inflation. Inflation. Inflation.
Resignation. Resignation. Resignation.
Absolution? Absolution? Absolution?

Places

Long before I came to live in the tiny city of Lichfield I was extremely fond of it as a place to visit. We passed through it on childhood trips to relatives in Derby and on occasions attended the Whitsuntide carnival that through the ages has been called 'The Bower'. By the 1980s, I had migrated as far East as Sutton Coldfield and was happy to travel a few miles further East to spend a Sunday afternoon now and then looking at the beautiful and uniquely three-spired cathedral founded by Saint Chad. The walls are adorned with statues of the Medieval Kings of England and of the Saints, including Chad. The spires, visible from miles around, are often known as the Ladies of the Vale.

To the South of the cathedral, leading to the oldest part of the city, around the market place adjacent to the Guild Church of Saint Mary, is Dam Street. After the cathedral itself, Lichfield is probably best known as the birthplace of Dr. Samuel Johnson. Streets and public houses are named after him, there is a statue of him and his biographer, Boswell, in the aforementioned market place and it is almost impossible to walk for two minutes inside the city boundary without seeing either his image or some other reference to him. What is the measure of reflected glory needed for a statue to be erected to the mere biographer of a great man? Boswell's work was of course of the highest standard but it is doubtful that he would have been commemorated as the biographer of anyone else. Friends of Johnson have shops and restaurants named after them and, on Dam Street there is Dame Oliver's house, as well as a shop named after her, in which she taught the young Samuel Johnson.

That is the backdrop to the 'Ballard of the Three Spires'

I wanted to write a poem in praise of the place in general and the cathedral in particular and the inspiration finally came from the most unlikely of sources. First World War poet, Ivor Gurney, wrote a piece called the 'Ballad of the Three Spectres' which I read one day and instantly had the title and theme for my poem.

However, an unexpected bonus came from Gurney's opening line *'As I went up by Ovillers'*. An Anglicised pronunciation of the battle-zone town in France sounds a lot like *'Oliver's'* and this gave me my own first line.

Ballad of the Three Spires

As I went past Dame Oliver's
on Dam Street, heading North,
in front of me there were three spires
who said "What is our worth?"

The South West one spoke through the moss.
"Our task is known to all!
We each support a golden cross,
without us they would fall"

"Well maybe so," her sister said,
"but surely there is more.
We point to where the Saints have led:
those Saints above the door"

The other spire spoke from the East.
"You're both right, friends, but wait.
Admiring eyes upon us feast:
not on Saint Peter's Gate"

Those Ladies of the Vale do me,
with all their charms, ensnare.
They need no task, for all can see
them standing, ever fair.

2006 was the 250th anniversary of the birth of Wolfgang Amadeus Mozart, the composer, of whom I have been a great admirer since 1971 when his work was drawn to my attention by the popularisation of part of his 40th Symphony by Waldo de los Rios. Partly for this reason, Denise and I decided to visit the region of his birth as part of a summer holiday. Rather than stay in Salzburg itself, although we did visit the Birthplace and other worthy sights, we stayed in the small town of St. Wolfgang, a few miles away and one of several towns and villages on the shores of a lake known as Wolfgangsee.

The general area is called Salzkammergut. The lake is overlooked by a mountain which, from some angles, has the look of a couchant lion. In the summer of 2007, in the footsteps of Wordsworth, I visited the lakes of Italy. However, Wolfgangsee and its surroundings remain the most serenely beautiful of the many places on Earth that I have had the good fortune to visit.

Another favourite place of mine, not particularly beautiful nor serene but delightful in other ways, is the town of Lagos in Portugal's Algarve. It has a church dedicated to the legend of a young man who, in temper, kicked his mother then, beside himself with remorse, removed the offending foot with an axe. An obliging local saint caused it to grow back and the rest, whilst not as they say being history, is a decent tale nonetheless.

Saint Wolfgang has a similar tale to tell. Wolfgang, after whom the musician was indirectly named by his mother, was a recluse of the first order. He lived in a cave up in the mountains and was in perpetual fear of Satan creeping up behind him and throwing him from his mountain lair into the lake. At last Wolfgang received Divine inspiration. He was to throw his axe as far as he could and, on the spot where it landed, he was to build a church. Successful completion of these tasks would guarantee eternal protection from Satan's threat. As luck would have it, in those days before coffer dams and underwater piling technology, the axe cleared the lake and landed on good ground where the church now stands.

Outside is a statue of the canonised Wolfgang holding his axe and gazing avuncularly on the lovely, lovely people of the town named after him and the equally lovely buildings in which they are fortunate enough to live and work. I hope they will forgive my teasing.

Salzkammergut

Lion Mountain lying,
proud but with no pride.
Singing breezes mingling
with birdsong at the side
of waters lapping at the shores,
from Strobl to St. Gilgen,
in time with music from the scores
by Mozart, sent from heaven.

Caring townsfolk sharing
their fayre with all who come.
Rendered houses tended
by those who are at home
in these small towns that draw us
from everywhere on Earth
to gaze like those before us.
Hear our joyous mirth!

Be-devilled hermit levelled
the land to build a church.
God-guided axe decided where
when thrown from lofty perch.
His wooden effigy now guards
the market place, the fountain
and sloping roofs with jerkin heads
in the shadow of his mountain.

During the visit to Salzkammergut, we had intended to make a day trip to Vienna. However, this proved to be too ambitious as an eighteen hour round trip from St. Wolfgang to Vienna via Salzburg would leave insufficient time to see more than a tiny fraction of what Vienna has to offer. As soon as we returned to England, therefore, we made arrangements to spend a few days in Vienna and we were fortunate enough to be joined on that adventure by my wonderful cousin Maureen and her husband Steve Potter. Staying, ironically, in the Hotel Beethoven, we toured Royal Palaces, Museums and Art Galleries. We stood and stared in awe at the Opera House and countless other buildings equally impressive and sampled the delights of a Mozart concert at the Hofburg as well as the wurst and torte at the Hotel Sacher. Unlike many major cities, Vienna was scrupulously clean and its people polite, friendly, helpful and inviting. They say that there is almost no crime in Vienna and, although they would say that to tourists, wouldn't they, I do believe them.

So is this Utopia? Has this city, that has been central to key historical events for centuries also achieved a state of perfection? Sadly, the answer is 'No!'. The people seem to share a habit of continuously smoking the foulest smelling cigarettes outside France. There are no apparent legal rules or social disapprovals to restrain them and the exquisite flavour of many a bowl of goulash was impaired by a smoker sitting nearby. Back home, in the clean air of Staffordshire, I wrote 'Rauchen Verboten' using a very large proportion of my total German vocabulary. In some cases the forty years passage of time since my last German lesson had served to diminish my always tenuous grasp of grammatically correct word endings but, there again, that applies to my English too!

The first part is addressed to the people of Vienna and the second to Vienna itself. At the end of the second line of the second stanza I used the word 'fuhrer'. I did this for two reasons. First, I recalled it as being the German word for 'leader' and, second, I wanted to say that the city and its people deserve the title that was taken for his own by that evil madman, Adolf Hitler. In checking and correcting my grammar, my old friend Dr. Gillian James suggested that I substitute a word I had never previously encountered, 'leiter'. Not only did this substitution remove any possibility of my poem unintentionally offending the very people I sought to extol but it also provided a useful half-rhyme with 'leute'. Thank you, Gill, for that and other improvements to my draft.

Rauchen verboten!

Rauchen nicht, meine wunderbare Leute
Ihr seid meine Freunde und meine Helden.
Eure Gebäude und Eure Kunst sind schon
Eure Geschichte und Eure Musik haben keine Überstehenden

O, Wein, ich liebe Dich und Deine Leute
Du bist meine Geliebte und unser Leiter
Deine Kinder sind meine Schwestern
und meine Brüder, ich will Euch immer lieben

Rauchet nicht sondern für immer leben!

Smoking is forbidden!

Do not smoke my wonderful people
You are my friends and my heroes
Your buildings and your art are beautiful
Your history and your music have no superior

Oh Vienna, I love you and your people
You are my beloved and our leader
Your children are my sisters
and my brothers, I will always love you.

Do not smoke but live forever!

Sometimes poems seem to write themselves as if freed, like the Genie of the Lamp, by the gentle rubbing of my pen between thumb and forefinger. Early in 2006, Denise and I were staying with Robert and Angela Rawsthorn at Afton Lodge where they lived, on the outskirts of Freshwater, Isle of Wight. The upper floors at Afton Lodge give amazing views of Tennyson Down from beyond the Monument to the distant ridge over Freshwater Bay and the Military Road. One evening we watched spellbound as thousands of rooks made continuously changing shapes in the fading light for what seemed like an hour before roosting in the nearby trees. Liz Rawsthorn, visiting her parents and us, thoughtfully provided us with the knowledge that one of the collective names for rooks is 'a building'. I must confess that I had thought that these were starlings until I was corrected by my friends.

Awake at dawn the following day, I was somehow reminded that it was the 200th anniversary of the birth of the great engineer, Isambard Kingdom Brunel. For me, Brunel is a contender, behind Isaac Newton, for the title of 'Greatest Ever Englishman'. One of the many reasons for my admiration is the fact that he managed to align the tunnel under Box Hill, Wiltshire in such a way that the rising sun shines through it from end to end every year on his birthday, 9th April. The Heel Stone at Stonehenge boasts a similar success at mid-summer but the sheer showmanship of Brunel in doing it for his own birthday sets him apart from the anonymous Druid (or was it an Ancient Egyptian?) who first came up with the idea of this type of link between building and Nature. Not limited to tunnels, Brunel also conquered the seas with huge metal ships such as S.S. Great Britain and designed marvellous bridges such as the one across Clifton Gorge, near Bristol. The Latin inscription in St. Paul's Cathedral in London declares it to be the monument to its designer, Sir Christopher Wren. I think of Brunel's work as performing a similar job for him.

Later the same morning I made the short journey to The Needles and to Freshwater Bay, as I never tire of seeing the rock formations. For many years Freshwater Bay was symbolised by a rock that had eroded to form an arch but this eventually collapsed in the 1990s, leaving just two which are known locally as Mermaid and Stag. These sights completed my poem 'Monuments' by giving it a spiritual feel which I think is as close as I am ever likely to get to the wonderful but as yet unpublished, 'Paradox' by Tina Negus.

Monuments

The ninth day of April, two thousand and six
Anno Domini, they used to say,
and I am early awake with the rising sun
through an unshaded window, reflecting.
Left bare to maintain my view of Tennyson Down,
foreshortened slumber a small price to pay for this sight:
little compares with this growing light.
The dawn chorus further stimulates my waking senses as did
the roosting of the rooks at the previous dusk,
a building of rooks some say.
This Afton is as sweet as any other, I think.

The top of Alfred's monument can just be seen, glistering
and that stirs my senses of history.
It is two hundred years since Brunel was born and,
as I muse, the same sun will shine
through one of the many monuments to that engineer:
all of his own building and design.
I speak of the tunnel 'neath Box
and the perfection of its creation which,
along with the ships and the spans,
makes a shrine this day for that man.

Then I rise and see the chalk ridge and the rocks,
Mermaid, Stag and Needles since Arch is no more,
and I picture Clifton Gorge and that hill and the mighty seas.
Are these all monuments, self-built, to Him?
I wonder.
Sometimes I just have to wonder.

By this stage, the name Tina Negus may have become familiar to the reader but it is time to add a few words of introduction to one of the major inspirations for this book as well as being a significant contributor. Tina is actually my second cousin although we have dispensed entirely with the full titles for each other; we are cousins.

She is a genuine polymath, a master of all trades (careful not to use the word 'mistress') and an accomplished artist with a scientific background and education. Pottery, painting and poetry are met with equal relish and she often combines the latter two to complement each other.

By the time that Tina and I met, we had shared not just Planet Earth but the same family for a combined total of 117 years. We had been separated by gender, geography and, in the early days, by age although from childhood until my early twenties I had been close to and fond of her parents. We had both been regular visitors to our mutual and much loved Great Aunt Eva but at different times.

Once we had established contact, by means described elsewhere in this book, I soon learned of her interest in poetry and this added impetus to my own life-long but occasionally dormant writings.

'Tara' is the first of several of her poems that she has permitted me to include. It needs no explanation beyond saying that its link with 'Gone with the Wind' is only indirect, almost remote in fact, but that its conservationist credentials are a welcome addition to this book.

It is followed by Tina's 'Lichfield Angel'. When I first received this one, through the post rather than by e mail which is our more usual form of communication, I naturally assumed from the title that it was about me! However, it turned out to have been written in response to a newspaper article that I had sent her about the discovery in Lichfield Cathedral of a sculpture that had been buried for several centuries.

By the time this book is published, the Angel should be on permanent display at the Cathedral. I do have some doubts about the story of its history as it seems to me to be very speculative indeed, but that is for possible future study.

Tara

Here it was that kings were crowned
To rule in majesty:
To hold in trust the holy ground,
Beneath the sacred tree.

And here they sang to burning fire
In May and Lammas-tide,
With pipe and drum and harp and lyre,
The darkness they defied.

This place is Ireland's ancient heart
That still keeps time today
With seasons' rhythms: set apart,
It's secret life and way.

Between the stones the king once rode
On horse and chariot swift,
To mythic bride in gods' abode
To cede the land in gift.

And all the people gathered here
Around the central hill,
From all the kingdoms, far and near,
Their duties to fulfil.

And is it true, what people say,
That this is what is planned?
To build a bloody motorway
Through Tara's magic land?

Tina Negus

Lichfield Angel

Beneath the sanctuary slabs,
an angel of light,
hidden in the dark,
buried deep,
forgotten.

Unearthed, during restoration,
this Saxon Gabriel,
with painted wings and curling hair,
announcing forever to a missing Mary,
the unlikely word.

Was he here when Chad was bishop?
Was he broken then?
Was he concealed to keep him safe?

Years, decades, centuries
he has lain within the confines of the choir,
unknown.

Now, revealed again,
in honour,
in splendour:
the Lichfield Angel.

Tina Negus (for Graham)

Louisa

In eighteen hundred and ninety-nine,
an event took place so brave that time
won't erode the record of men so fine
that Englishmen can be proud of.
A storm blew up the like of which
had ne'er been seen; neither poor nor rich
could recall such a time when the Gods did stitch
the sea to the sky with such hatred.

Hatred, hatred, when the Gods did stitch the sea to the sky with such hatred.

The "Forrest Hall" did carry away;
dragging her anchor across the bay.
If help don't come, they be history today;
leaving their wives and their sweethearts.
The cry for help down the wire did shout,
and the Cox'n knew there was no doubt
that when the rocket called them out
to Louisa's house, all would hasten.

Hasten, hasten, when the rocket called them out to Louisa's house all would hasten

The wind did roar and the sea did crash;
o'er harbour wall, the waves did smash
and reduced the lighthouse flame to ash,
so a Lynmouth launch was doomed.
Doomed to fail; no chance to try;
To stand and leave the barque to die;
But the Cox'n did give out the cry
"We launch from Porlock Weir".

"We launch from Porlock Weir".
he cried, and with good cheer
they pushed and shoved; their faces grim;
they pulled the ropes and hauled with him;
it's a hell of a pull to Porlock Weir.

They pushed and shoved and did their best;
they knew the sailors be distressed;
if Louisa don't get there, they be guests
in Davy Jones' back locker.
The wind did blast; the rain did pour,
They thought they'd died, but pulled some more,
they were blasted by the mighty roar
of the gale that hated and thrashed them.

Thrashed them, thrashed them; blasted by the mighty roar
of the gale that hated and thrashed them.

Lashed by winds, the men were soaked
they heaved and hauled and pulled the boat;
for 13 miles them Lynmouth folk
did haul Louisa to launch her.
And when to shore they did at last
achieve their goal and rig the mast
and launched, and with their hearts steadfast
did pull for the "Forrest Hall".

"We launch from Porlock Weir".
he cried, and with good cheer
they pushed and shoved; their faces grim;
they pulled the ropes and hauled with him;
it's a hell of a pull to Porlock Weir.

They pulled their oars with all their breath,
though waves struck fear into their chests,
and snatched the sailors from their deaths
on the rocks of the waiting coastline.
One hundred years have passed since then
but lifeboatmen still know that when
the call to launch shall come again,
they will; and not for the fiver !

"We launch from Porlock Weir".
he cried, and with good cheer
they pushed and shoved; their faces grim;
they pulled the ropes and hauled with him;
it's a hell of a pull to Porlock Weir.

by
John M.D. Bacon and Jean M. Bacon

John and Jean are old and dear friends. Sometime in the late 1990s Denise and I had arranged to spend a weekend in Canterbury during which we had tickets to see the folk duo 'Show of Hands' in an open air concert nearby. We had first encountered this duo at the Fylde Festival with John and Jean a year or two earlier. As a surprise, I think it was for my birthday, Denise had arranged for John and Jean to join us and, over dinner on the first evening, they gave me a copy of 'Louisa' which they had co-written with the intention of having it set to music as a folk song to commemorate the centenary in 1999 of the remarkable launch of the Lynmouth life boat. This ten ton beast was manhandled up and then down 1 in 4 hills reaching a height of 1423 feet, over a distance of 13 miles in the dark to achieve a safe launch and attend the gale-damaged Forrest Hall. A copy was given to Steve Knightley, songwriter and lead vocalist with Show of Hands, who is interested in all things that are West Country related but who has not yet, to the best of my knowledge, added 'Louisa' to their repertoire. As a New Year gift at their family house in 2007 John and Jean gave me permission to include it here. One day **I** shall give it a tune.

After nearly 25 years of membership of the Institution of Civil Engineering Surveyors, it became 'Buggins' turn' and I was elected President for the year 1997/98. I had been an active member spasmodically during those years but the jury is still out as to whether I was given the honour because they thought I deserved it or because they needed to fill a gap until a better candidate was free. Either way, it was an interesting year although it came and went with me being frustrated in my thwarted attempts to alter certain things in sea-change proportions. The lesson I learned by the experience was that the art of subtle persuasion rather than dynamic leadership is the way to make things happen. The year was not without its high spots and humorous incidents, one of these occurring one Sunday morning when Denise was telling her mother that we were going to Hong Kong for a while. In an attempt to explain why, she came out with the immortal expression 'Graham isn't just President in this country, he is President of the World'. It became a catch–phrase and gave me a private sense of superiority over US President Bill Clinton when he visited the Midlands during our co-incident terms of office! Hong Kong was most enjoyable and we were among the last to fly into Kai Tak airport with its notorious 90 degree approach turn during which we seemed to be weaving between high rise apartment blocks in which we could see the occupants waving at us. The tour we did of the almost complete but not yet open Chep Lap Kok airport, including a drive down the runway, was also a rare treat. It has become a tradition for I.C.E.S Presidents to visit Professor Chen at Shenzhen School of Surveying, to exchange views on the profession and to show support for the many Chinese members of I.C.E.S. We are always well looked after by Professor Chen and his colleagues but it does involve a trip up into Mainland China from Kow Loon. The journey on the Mass Transit Railway could not fail to make one wonder how they can be so clean, efficient and punctual whilst transporting much larger numbers of passengers than their UK counterparts. In many restaurants that we visited, pictures of the recently departed last Governor of Hong Kong, Chris Patten, still hung on the walls. It was clear that the ex-pat community still had a Colonial mentality with every intention of sending their children back to Blighty for schooling, most retaining homes there as possible future bolt-holes. A certain mind-set is needed to live and work abroad and I wondered, in the event that these people had to leave Hong Kong as it became re-absorbed into China, whether they would be able to settle back home. Perhaps they would have to find 'new territories' elsewhere.

East is West

I went to China for the day,
a feat that may sound strange
for one who lives in Staffordshire,
with flying to arrange.

Shenzhen is further than Shenstone,
you'd say and you'd be right,
but when you start from Hong Kong town
you do not need a flight.

Mass Transit is the way to go,
from Kow Loon to Shenzhen,
it leaves on time, you have a seat,
not herded in a pen.

To meet Professor Chen was fun,
he must be tired of us,
as year by year we visit him,
he always makes a fuss.

A Malta with Manhattan mix,
is what I called Hong Kong,
a 'must-see' once or twice, perhaps,
if you can stand the throng.

We hired it for a hundred years,
before they took it back,
now better placed to lose our rent,
we'd set them on their track.

Presidents come and Gov'nors go,
Chris Patten was the last,
What will become of Hong Kong now,
will ex-pats be out cast?

When they return to Solihull,
to Wilmslow or to Slough,
will they still think their life is full,
or need another, now?

The English Lake District continues to fill me with mixed feelings.

For me, it is in a league above Cornwall, the Peak District and the Yorkshire Dales as far as scenery is concerned although at least Cornwall does have the sea. At the same time, it is a poor relation of equivalent regions throughout Europe and North America. I include the Scottish Lochs in the latter category.

On separate visits to Windermere, Grasmere, Coniston, Rydal Water and such, I have been disappointed one minute and awe-struck the next: maybe that is why the region is, and has been for two centuries, so popular. I suspect that the connection with William Wordsworth and his friends has helped the tourist industry more than a little.

It was on one of my more inspired days during a stay at Grasmere's Red Lion Hotel that 'Lakeland Spring' was written. It is not only about Grasmere but also about neighbouring towns, hills and lakes, as well as taking into account the paths and tracks that link them. Those circular section chimney stacks that abound in the region are charming and seem to soften the otherwise hard edges of the local architecture. From some angles the diminishing courses of the tiled roofs can have the effect of blurring the ridge line from the hills beyond. Harmony with Nature, unbeatable!

There is absolutely no need to explain any further the physical features, man-made as well as natural, that are referred to in these blank verses.

What is interesting is that, as with 'Monuments', a sort of spiritual theme forces its way into the last few lines. I have no idea who wrote the Christmas song 'I saw three ships' and I am fairly sure that no-one else does either. However, I am grateful to Graham Hancock for the phrase 'heaven's mirror', although the one he referred to in his book of the same name is about fifteen hundred miles to the East of mine and much drier.

Lakeland Spring

Snow covered hill-tops catch the Sun of Spring,
first give the nether-bracken, brown and mauve,
the iridescence of a starling's chest
then the lived-in look of a threadbare rug.

Walls of rough-cut stone mark the rising banks
like laughter-lines upon a frowning face.
They doubtless have another purpose too;
perhaps to separate the flocks of sheep.

Slated roofs in diminishing courses
surmount the sturdy walls of clean-hewn stone,
are drained by dated gutters of cast-iron
and to round, smokeless chimneys are lead-flashed.

And now the morning mists appear in layers,
some glowing bright as fibre-optic ends,
but some still dull, awaiting random rays
of sun through clouds that cloak the entire scene.

Sombre and naked hollow trees survive
another season, leafless but alive
and soon shall show another coat of green
to complement the eager daffodils.

Icy puddles crackle beneath the feet
that walk in wonder down the coffin path
with startled, grey-fleeced sheep, their faces black,
their eyes, reflective green, like those of cats.

Translucent waves conceal the paddles of
the easy glide of swans upon the lake,
advancing backwards in the forceful flow.
It matters not, there is nowhere to go.

The cob and pen and cygnet sail on by
like those three ships upon a Christmas morn.
And who do we think could have made such ships,
is this, on calmer days, like Heaven's mirror?

The Steeple

Stark against the wintry sky
above the trees forlorn,
the lofty steeple towers high
waiting for the dawn.

The scudding clouds that race above
look down with carefree eye.
Look down without a sign of love
to where our forebears lie.

What action will the morrow bring
within this churchyard gaunt?
Will another join the ring
that round the tombstones haunt?

Will a cortege wind its way
along the curling path;
then inside the church to pray
for Death's cold aftermath.

Or shall we hear the wedding bell
peal forth across the way?
The smiling couple cannot tell
how long they'll see the day.

No matter what the action be,
the impassive steeple stands.
A mute spectator, caring not
for what this life demands.

Brian H. Woodall c.1953

One of my great passions is the consumption of astonishing quantities of red wine, particularly the many varieties from Australia but these are too strong, really, so I tend to stay with the French. Although the wine from Bardolino is not among my favourites, I have been known to sample it on more than one occasion. During a trip to Italy's Lake Garda I called in at Bardolino and so, unfortunately for me, did thousands of others to crowd the many shops, bars and restaurants.

The lake provides a tolerable view to gaze upon over a leisurely lunch – there is no option about it being leisurely as the waiters are the slowest outside Jamaica – except that from many restaurants the views are obscured by lines of people jockeying for position before the next ferry comes in. Not the English, of course, we form orderly queues and sometimes miss the boat as a result! All the time in that part of the World, ear drums are threatened by high-revving but very small capacity motor cycles and scooters.

The highlight of the town for me was actually the war memorial which comprises a granite obelisk engraved with the names of local men who died in the World Wars of the twentieth century, surrounded at its base by a heavy steel chain supported at each corner by large shell cases positioned like the lions in Trafalgar Square.

Italy, of course, entered both of the World Wars of the twentieth century relatively late. Nowhere near as late as the Americans were but certainly later than the 'regulars' like England, Germany and Austria. To the Italians the World Wars were dated 1915 –18 and 1940-45.

To embellish the obelisk further are the figures of two men looking less like modern warriors than they do ancient combatants. Or is one simply supporting a fallen colleague?

Either way it is a dramatic sculpture and in the hand of the surviving fighter is what appears to be the gladius of his ancestors with which he is engraving Owen's (or Horace's) 'old lie' Pro Patria............

I was moved to write a short sonnet sequence which I have called simply 'Bardolino I and II'.

Bardolino

I

In Bardolino there is more than wine
to entertain the tourists for a day:
a thousand bars and restaurants form a line,
as well as shops galore, to make them pay.
Before they came, the lake was there for years,
with distant mountains adding to the view.
Now peace is shattered by the screech of gears,
the vista hidden by the ferry queue

But near the town there is a monument
to men from S.Alberti to Zanetti
It covers both the wars where they were sent
to die with Andreoli and Zucchelli.
It seems the townsfolk are, like us, content
to let their men die, alphabetically

II

A granite obelisk with rocket fins
stands at the lakeside on the edge of town
A million tourists neither smile nor frown
as war is war, whichever nation wins.
Around the base, an anchor chain is borne
By timeless, nameless shells which, set four-square,
sit like Nelson's lions around his lair.
His triumph once was lauded as a dawn

The start and finish dates of both World Wars
are closer here than by that other lake.
Still time enough to lose men to a cause,
in Latin stated 'for their country's sake'.
Victor and vanquished disobey time's laws
but use a gladius 'the lie' to make.

Living as I do in land-locked Lichfield, for me to get to Garda it was necessary to take a short flight to Verona from Birmingham and then a bus ride of about twenty miles during which I was able to see at least some of the city which I understand was largely made famous by William Shakespeare.

I am not a great fan of the Bard although I concede that he was rather more than the 'over-rated medieval scribbler' that I once described him as being to my stunned luncheon colleagues at the Rotary Club in Lichfield. At one 'Parents' Evening' some years ago, my daughter's English teacher clearly didn't share my opinion either and very politely filed me away mentally under 'Philistine'. I understand that a couple of his plays, including 'Romeo and Juliet' were set in Verona and I have no doubt that the enterprising locals charge handsomely to see the balcony from which Miss Capulet made her speech, whether or not there ever was such a balcony or, for that matter, a Miss Capulet.

What I saw was row upon row of apartment blocks, each with row upon row of elevated walkways at every level, each comprising concrete decks and simple steel parapet fences, unlike the ornately carved stonework that one envisages as supporting the balcony above Master Montague's young and expectant head.

I have no idea who the 'two gentlemen' were, nor where they lived and in what arrangement of relationship.

The streets through which we drove were remarkably clean and tidy, with freshly painted buildings down each side, all roofed in what I know as Roman tiles. As this particular fragment of learning came to me at college in England I should not have been surprised to see such tiles in Verona as well, both having been part of the Roman Empire.

My intention was to return to Verona for a day during my visit to the region but I didn't find the time and so I must arrange another visit one day. Who knows, perhaps such a visit would inspire even me to write a play set on its streets and concrete walkways

Until then, yet another sonnet, deliberately not in Shakespearean style, will have to sum up my brief encounter with Verona

Verona

In Verona many a scene is set.
Fact or fiction? I neither know nor care.
There are a thousand balconies but yet
not one deserving of a maiden, fair.
The well-swept streets with buildings are twice lined,
clean and painted, like an exhibition,
and roofed with Roman tiles, how odd to find
these so far North. But, perhaps, tradition
gives them the name from Empire days, long gone,
ere Garibaldi gave us Italy
and several kings a throne to sit upon
before the fall of that brief monarchy.
My visit here was briefer still, soon gone.
I shall return to learn its history

'New Jersey' was written one afternoon in Lyndhurst, New Jersey, when I should have been writing something much more cerebral.

Sometime in the early 1990s, after years of managing construction projects, I enrolled, for reasons long since forgotten if ever known, on a post-graduate course in Construction Project Management. In turn, this led me to spend a couple of weeks which included my forty third birthday studying American techniques in Manhattan. Also for unknown reasons, we actually stayed in Lyndhurst, commuting to New York for meetings and site visits whilst attending lectures and performing various tasks and assignments back at the hotel.

A small group comprising Roger Pearce, Mary Morrisey, Adam Westwood and I arrived a few days before the rest and left a day or so after they did. This extra time gave us the opportunity to see the sights to the extent that they could stimulate our interest and it is with enduring regret that although this did include the exteriors of the World Trade Centre and the Empire State Building, we did not, and now never shall in the case of the former, go inside. At least not to the upper floors. Less than a decade later, the 'Twin Towers' had gone!

We took pleasure in buying gifts for those at home from the famous Macey's department store, except for Roger who scored his 'Brownie Points' at a discount. The question as to why the Empire State Building was so-called arose one day, as it had been built in the 1920s when **the** Empire was already on its last legs and as New York had never been part of it anyway. Most American States have nicknames such as 'garden' 'sunshine' and 'lone star' so we assumed (correctly as it happens) that New York is the Empire State. I vaguely recalled from a cigarette packet nearly thirty years earlier that New York was previously called New Amsterdam and so maybe the name was connected with the Dutch Empire. Nonsense of course but it occupied us until we reached the disappointingly unremarkable Wall Street from the top corner of which we gazed in awe of the 'Twin Towers' and tried hard to capture the scene on camera. Mary, a good Catholic girl, was more interested in acquiring a picture of Saint Patrick's Cathedral for her mother.

Throughout our stay, only Adam from our group gave the course the attention it deserved. For most of us it was a holiday, paid for but earned only in part by a few days' study.

New Jersey

I'm forty three but feeling half of that
here in New Jersey in the Summertime.
We went to Macey's shop, named on the mat
and on the bags, for which they charge a dime.
But Roger bought his bargains on the Mall
and, from the trash can by the deli bar,
he took a wrapper. Yes, he had the gall,
to stow in it a cheapskate perfume jar!
"Why *Empire State*?" remained a mystery
as on to Wall Street and those Towers we walked.
I wondered if it came from Dutch history
but only of Saint Patrick's, Mary talked.
My room-mate, Adam, faithful to the course
that took us there, the rest had no remorse.

The 2006 trip to the Isle of Wight from which 'Monuments' emerged will also be remembered for the events of one afternoon a few miles inland.

Apart from her poetry and painting, Tina Negus is also a keen photographer with a special interest in church architecture or, more specifically embellishments. When she heard that I was to visit the Island she asked me to pop along to the church at Shalfleet and take a photograph for her of the entrance door. It was not the door itself that particularly interested her but the carving on what I would have lazily called the fanlight above it. Actually, it is a tympanum although I have used a bit of licence in the poem that follows and referred to it as an arch, for reasons which will be apparent. In truth, it is the bit between the arch and the horizontal head of the door.

Anyway, this particular tympanum is of stone and is carved to display a male figure with a couple of generic animals at his side. Not unnaturally, in my opinion, I took this to be the Biblical character, Noah, leading his charges aboard the Ark two at a time. I was wrong. Tina happened to be writing a learned paper on another Biblical character at that time and informed me that my man was obviously Daniel and that the two animals were lions.

We left Shalfleet and went for a walk in the hills around Shorwell (which rhymes with coral) probably calling in the Crown Inn for a pint of beer as we usually do. One of these hills is called Mount Ararat and it was covered in a layer of greenery which Angela informed us was wild garlic. As she bent to pick up a handful to find which if any part of the plant had the familiar smell of garlic, a movement a few inches from her outstretched hand caught her eye and she saw it was a female adder. I was next to her and a whisper went down the line through Denise to Rob who, as always on walks, takes a large lead because of his long legs. The snake reared its head, poised to strike and, for a few moments the only movement was Rob's unsuccessful attempt to take his camera from a back pocket.

Despite being a highly qualified nurse, Angela suffers badly with bee stings and the like so, although the resultant poem was written with a large measure of humour, it could easily have been a very serious incident.

The Angel and the Snake

Near Shorwell's Crown this Ararat was climbed
with thoughts of Noah's arch on Shalfleet's door
still dwelling, soon to be much later timed,
with Daniel and his lions to the fore.

Among the garlic leaves an Angel trod
then stooped, their wild aroma to inhale.
Alert, she saw the rising of a rod
once coiled and now erect, but not the male.
Those Hellish fangs and diamond back were clear
and, for a moment, terror struck her dumb.
Amidst all living things, when Death is near
an earthly Angel knows her time has come.

But, all the while, the snake was filled with fear
and turned to slip away. That is the sum.

Sometime in the mid 1970s I heard BBC Radio presenter, Johnnie Walker, read an account of life as it was for the Native North Americans during the nineteenth century when all kinds of atrocities were inflicted upon them by European settlers. Since then I have had great respect for those people and this was enhanced a few years later when I heard a proverb which translates roughly as 'The mountains laugh when they see men fighting over who owns them'.

Eventually, these thoughts inspired a poem which, as is very frequently the case, was started then stalled after a stanza or two. In more recent times the matter of climate change has become more and more a news item with the current thinking of the so-called experts being that by some means the human population of this planet has been able to change the environment more dramatically in two centuries than it was able to do for itself in millions of years.

As far as I can see, the internal combustion engine and the jet engine are the main scapegoats for an alleged act of murder when, as yet, no body has been found.

In trying to make some sense of all this, it occurred to me that my old North American friends may have unwittingly stumbled upon another truth. The proverb was obviously intended to refer to the take-over of land by one type of people from another, in that case Europeans from Native Americans. However, the same could clearly be said of the eventual take-over by Homo Sapiens from Tyrannosaurus Rex and his subjects and I wonder if the same can be said of the ultimate take-over bid – when, in the process of fighting each other, all the Nations of the World are united in defeating Earth itself.

Personally, I still have 'reservations' (sorry about the pun) about the consensus view of scientists as the recent changes may still yet prove to be cyclical as always before. However, if it is eventually shown to be true, and if our human activities really do end up having the potency to make a significant change to the planet, then it will be a Pyrrhic victory with the defeated mountains still laughing over the corpses of the men who achieved it.

Climate change

I love to hear the mountains laugh
as men do battle at their feet.
What arrogance those microbes have
if they believe they own the peak.

For years unnumbered, hills have stood
and worn the clouds like coronets.
The flower of Man was not yet bud
when Earth gave forth those monoliths.

If permafrost becomes a bog
and mighty icebergs melt away,
can this be just because the fog
from Man's machines destroyed the sky?

For what is Man, how long has he
held court upon a global throne?
A day or less, compared to thee,
Oh Mother Nature, all alone.

Throughout your reign the ice has been
and gone again a hundred times.
Without the fossil fuels, my Queen,
would you stand guilty of these crimes?

And did the King of Lizards plot
to make his monarchy so brief
by living life the way he ought,
his only power those awesome teeth.

Should Daimler, Whittle and their kind,
accessories before the fact,
stand trial with Man, become enjoined
in charges made, their works knocked back?

We're as we are, we're of our age,
does not the Earth still spin and turn?
And so it shall on every page
of history, we shall come to learn.

Family

Immediately prior to a holiday near Newquay in Cornwall with my friend Martin Round and his then wife, Susan, my then wife, Patricia, announced that she was expecting our first child. We had been married for over two years but for a long time before then I had carried the usual young man's fear of hearing those words!

This was entirely different and I was instantly filled with a sense of pride that has never left me since.

A little out-pouring of emotion during the holiday worried me for an hour or two until Susan, a Registered Nurse, explained the effect of hormone changes on women. Or at least she explained to me that there were such things as hormone changes in women, I cannot claim to this day to understand them!

Right from the very start I was convinced that I was to have a son although we did discuss girls' names briefly. The baby was due in February and, as my paternal grandfather, Harold Claude, was born in that month I thought that Hayley Clare would give a daughter his initials as a tribute.

For a boy, we liked the name Stephen but a cousin of mine with that name had died in an accident, aged 17, only a couple of years earlier and I thought that his brother or sister may wish to name their future offspring after him or, perhaps, 'retire' the name in his memory. Eventually my lad was named after the Duke of York who, as Prince Andrew, had also been born in the month of February.

'Fatherhood' was written in a site hut in Oswestry in the Autumn of 1979 and without any conscious awareness of the connections of that town to Wilfred Owen; he was born there in 1893. Ironically, I was there in connection with the demolition and partial re-development of a former army camp albeit one connected more with the Second World War than with the First.

The poem was revised slightly in late 1982 using a portable typewriter and at that time I also wrote 'For Catherine' with the intention of reading both at the joint baptism of my two children; not in church but at the party we held at home afterwards. However, a day of excessive celebration fuelled by gallons of my home-made wine, got in the way and both poems were consigned to the attic where they have stayed until now.

You may read later that my mother had a superstition based upon the proverb about counting chickens before they are hatched. I now hold to this very strongly myself and had clearly moved to that view by early 1982 as, although I knew that I must write a poem for my second child, as I had done for the first (a desire for equality or equivalence that I maintain to this day) I would not tempt fate by doing so before she had been safely delivered.

I do not recall where the name Catherine came from although she took her middle name, Ann, from her mother. However, I did expect her to become known as Kate. That happened at her own behest but only for about a fortnight circa 1992.

She was born on a Sunday morning early in the Football Season and early enough in the day for me to play football or, more significantly, to announce to my team-mates the actual birth-weight, upon which they had been running a sweep. She weighed in at 8lb 2oz and, fittingly, her Uncle Phil was the closest and took the kitty.

My parents were delighted with the boy/girl completeness of the family, with Mom actually pointing out that I had done exactly the same as Dad. I think I know what she meant! My sister, Lucy, already had the full set by then and the fact that her daughter, Donna, had arrived before her son, Paul, added to the symmetry and balance by virtue of the gender difference between Lucy and I.

My dear mother had the ability to make everything in life seem rational and easily explained.

At the time of writing neither of my children has made so bold as to turn me into a grandfather although both have indicated an eventual intention to do so. If and when either or both do, I shall of course be delighted despite my falsely professed dislike of children between 5 and 15. It is only the badly-behaved ones in restaurants that I object to and I blame their parents anyway. My kids were great. I can only wish Andrew and Cathy and their respective partners the same symmetry and balance, and at least equal good fortune to that with which I have been blessed, in the quality and quantity of their own offspring.

Fatherhood

I can't believe that, after all these years,
I feel so proud that I shall be a dad.
His mom has sometimes shed some gentle tears.
"Just hormones," Sue says, "she is really glad"
I say 'his' with no doubt in me at all.
Some feeling deep inside me knows it's male
but, make no bones about this, I'd stand tall
to raise a little girl, her name I'd hail.

Stephen or Hayley, what shall be your name?
Her Majesty gave birth that time of year,
perhaps, for that, we'll call you just the same.
Andrew, you'd be, but you shall be no Peer.
So, son of mine, I shall teach you the game
and, when you're older, we shall share some beer.

For Catherine

I couldn't write this verse before you came.
I wish I had but never would tempt fate.
For sure, I would have loved you still the same
if you had been a boy and not my Kate.

My mom and dad produced the perfect set,
they shook my hand and kissed me for that match.
And Uncle Phil was pleased to win the bet,
on your birth weight, his winnings he would snatch!

It must be said, you are a lovely girl,
bonny and blithe and very full of grace,
perhaps, one day, your locks will show a curl.
If not, who cares? You are so fair of face.

And so my darling, Catherine, let me say
I'll be your rock forever, if I may.

I have mentioned 'Friends Reunited' earlier but that web-site has a spin-off which is now called 'Genes Reunited'. Thanks to my father's cousin, Brian, I have a detailed and extensive record of that side of my family and I entered much of that information onto the web-site at an early stage. I regularly receive enquiries from people sharing names with members of my family tree and one such enquiry came in early 2005 from Jennifer Bullimore who wanted to know about Stanley Batty. I explained that he had been married to a cousin of my father and that all I really knew about him, apart from the fact that he was a really nice chap, was that he used to live in Grantham and had two daughters, Tina and Gillian. Within minutes, Jen replied to my e mail message saying that she was in fact making the enquiry on behalf of the self-same Tina who was her life-long friend. Minutes later I received the first of what will eventually be a million messages from Tina herself. Her first thought was that I might be a previously unknown half-brother from a relationship that may have pre-dated the marriage of her parents: her mother was ten years her father's junior. However, the picture very soon became clear.

Tina and I just had to meet. She then lived in Grantham, where she had been born, but had lived within 20 miles of me for over 30 years. I had known this and had intended for most of that time to present myself at her house on one of the countless occasions that I passed within yards of it. We arranged to meet somewhere between our current abodes, and a place just south of Derby, from where our common ancestors hailed, was chosen.

My father Dennis and his cousin Brian came along, together with all our respective partners. We spent an afternoon looking at old photographs and comparing almost forgotten memories. I was later able to establish that a lady called Dorothy who had contacted me to say that she thought her husband Desmond Woodall was descended from my great great great grandparents, Mathew and Susannah, was mistaken although I strongly suspect that there will prove to be a blood link a little further back.

We all resolved to meet at least annually and we bettered the first attendance figure in 2006 with my third cousin Beryl and her husband Peter joining us. Meeting her has opened up another rich vein of relatives, some in Australia, with whom I hope to become acquainted in due course.

Swarkestone

Two leagues to the south of the Willn Street home
and five score years have passed.
The scions of Walter, Harold and Alfred are come
for each to meet each at last.

Only pictures from Leslie, for there was no son,
and Eva's did not endure
those decades whilst separate lives were run
and reunions were never sure.

The seed of Old Walter, with Louisa's blood,
flows through every vein
whilst they embrace, and talk, and choose the food
and drink that will them sustain.

Did Dennis know Tina when she was in youth,
or is it Margaret he means?
And of Ruffy the dog, oh, what is the truth?
Did she know him only from scenes?

Brian and Graham have been troubled by news,
from Dot who is married to Des,
that Mathew wed Mary when Susannah, we knew,
was his wife, the certificate says.

The afternoon flew, no-one noticed the rain,
and pictures were taken to keep
of the time that they met, and they will meet again
as love and blood both still run deep.

As a child I was enormously close to and very fond of my cousins. There were six of them, two of which I remember being born, with Robert being so named at my insistence. All came from my mother's siblings, Bert, Ernest and Norman Cooksey as my father was an only child. With my innate senses of equality and symmetry I always wished that I had Woodall cousins too and I have therefore been very happy to embrace Brian's children as such. Until Judith arrived in 1966 I had only Brian himself and another Robert, son of my Great Aunt Eva, to fill the gap and both were too much older than me to be truly regarded as equals within the family hierarchy.

Stephen, the youngest of the Cooksey cousins, was tragically killed in a car crash when he was seventeen and the oldest, Sylvia, died a couple of years later of a heart condition of which I had previously been oblivious. Before then, at the age of thirty, my 'Woodall' Robert (whose surname was actually Birch) had been killed in a railway accident. The surviving Robert was always great fun and the source of a great deal of kindness to all family members. However, he succeeded in staying single until he was nearly fifty when he took us all by surprise by marrying, with very little advance notice, a girl twenty years younger. David and I were as close as brothers for thirty years until our marriages and the advent of our respective offspring progressively reduced the amount of time we had available to spend together. A little over a year older than me and always much larger, Dave was a massive influence on my development, a contribution for which I shall always be grateful. Patricia and Maureen were like sisters and deserve greater mention than I give them but I needed to save their names for the end.

As Judith was joined by Victoria, Charlotte and eventually Matthew, a sense of family symmetry was beginning to emerge although it was to take several more years for them to reach ages at which the difference between us was immaterial. I am now close to and very fond of them all and with the added bonus of Tina coming into my life and with her sister Gillian at least in contact, it was time for a poem. The Latin title is, as you may by now guess, another tribute to Wilfred Owen but this one goes still further. It is a sort of double sonnet written in a form that very closely follows 'Dulce et Decorum Est'. The last line is a conveniently appropriate version of 'Pro Patria Mori' using the names of my two surviving Cooksey girl cousins. Corny? Contrived? Yes, guilty on both counts but who cares?

Consobrini mei

Numerically speaking, I had six
but two of Dad's produced the same again.
A dozen cousins is the current mix,
with more I hope to meet, I know not when.
Three girls like older sisters were to me
when we were young, but Sylvie grew not old
and Stephen, younger still, was first to see
the side of life that's better, so we're told.

Our Robert was for years a Peter Pan
who often speaks his mind but can be coy
and David and Goliath are one man,
a giant and my mentor. As a boy
he kept me free from harm and helped me plan
my life, my work and all that brought me joy.

Now I turn to those of paternal traits,
four known since they were born and two found late.

In truth our Gill is still unseen by me,
it will be sweet for us to meet one day.
But Tina shares my love of poetry
and is an artist too, with paint and clay.
The other four are closer on the map
(I speak of Charlotte, Vicky, Matt and Jude)
and younger but, with cousins, there's no gap
as ages are just numbers wrongly viewed.
So there you see them all, I've named the rest
of those that bring our forebears lasting glory.
But two more names I give with no less zest
Patricia and Maurie.

In 1975 the English political scene was grim to say the least. After what he always called 'thirteen years of Tory misrule' Harold Wilson just about managed to wrest power from a debilitated Conservative Party in 1964. Although returned as Prime Minister in 1974 after a four year interruption by Edward Heath, he was coming to the end of his period of power. The secret of his return to power was neither his ability nor his potential but the votes cast by a reluctant electorate which would clearly have preferred an old style, dependable Tory leader if there had been one around. Heath never had the charisma and a significant number of voters were undoubtedly influenced by Johnny Speight's Alf Garnett referring to him as a 'Grammar School Twit'. Us Grammar School Twits preferred him to a politically misguided academic but there were too few of us to carry the vote, a situation partly created and certainly perpetuated by the cutting off of the supply of new 'twits' as Grammar School after Grammar School was closed. But there were a few of us left and one of these had the advantage of being a girl. Margaret Thatcher successfully challenged for Heath's leadership of the Conservative Party and with Wilson gone and his avuncular but even more inept successor, James Callaghan unable to cling to power any longer, despite the help of the desperate-for-any-credibility Liberal Party, she became Prime Minister in 1979. Known as the 'Iron Lady', she did not suffer fools gladly and during her eleven years or so as Premier she succeeded in consigning the anachronistic trade union movement to a generation or more of emasculation. She introduced fairer income tax rates to encourage effort and initiative. She fought hard to make the rating system fair by introducing a charge equal for all persons although this was sabotaged by the Press which branded it 'a poll tax' (as if there would have been anything wrong with that) and she led the country to war with Argentina when its leader had the temerity to invade our outpost in the Falkland Islands as a diversion from his domestic crises. Margaret was born and raised in Grantham but for at least twenty years before I had even heard of her, 'Margaret of Grantham' was the name given to a cousin of my father to distinguish her from many other Margarets in the family. She was for us the personification of good taste and sophistication. The World was a better place when both ladies were in their prime.

'Gemini??' (with double question marks to play down my twinning of these two paragons) was written on a train from Lichfield to London, the journey and the composition taking precisely the same amount of time.

Gemini ??

The name of which I speak was known to all.
It was the cause of loathing, fear and scorn
but only from the scoundrels who did fall
beneath the iron hand, do not **them** mourn.

To others it meant help, relief, reward
and fairer tax on income and the poll.
Defeat to Galtieri and his horde
was handed out as wetter heads did roll.

By me the name was known before the rest.
It meant sophistication in all ways,
like eating eggs the way that is the best,
with cousins to be found in later days.

What **is** the name? It should be clear by now,
Margaret of Grantham: both are missed, and how!

My mother, Dorothy, was known by most as Dot although her brother, Ernest, always called her Doris. My little sister was Christened Lynda but I have always called her Lucy so that must be a thing that big brothers do.

Mom was perpetually unfortunate. She was the fourth child and only daughter born in the depressed inter-war years in the same house as several other family members including me, some 23 years later, and Lucy three years after that - a day I remember very well. When Mom was ten years old her father was killed in an industrial accident which, these days, would probably make his widow a millionairess but which certainly did not at that time. Mom's three brothers were soon called away to war but by rare good fortune they all survived the hostilities.

Her education was severely restricted by the family situation, by her gender and by the Luftwaffe which often caused loss of sleep during nights in a shelter which had to be made up during what should have been lesson time at school the next day. It was not restricted by her intellect. She had a good brain and an amazing ability to work out explanations for almost everything that life threw at her.

However, not all of her solutions were based upon fact as she was a lady of many superstitions. Her expression 'Don't have a black heart' still carries me through difficult times, meaning simply that to hold a grudge against someone achieves nothing more than to preserve and reiterate the offence that caused it. Against her wise counsel I once changed the date on my bedside calendar to show the correct date when I awoke the next morning. There could have been no other possible explanation for Karen Withers sinking her newly acquired and still sharp front teeth into my upper arm at school the next day. At no time in the half-century since, have I knowingly repeated the mistake.

Mom's answer to any question on history was 'Thomas á Becket' and her grasp of foreign languages more or less began and ended with an expression used by an older work colleague at Messrs Adams and Benson Ltd where she was gainfully employed until her confinement with me. She suffered ill health for much of her life, especially after a seven month hospital stay in 1957/1958 as a result of the tuberculosis epidemic of that time.

However, she was able to enjoy the relative comfort of her own house, a family car (although she never drove) and holidays both abroad and in England during the second half of her life, including many in a 'continental frame tent' which was state of the art camping for the middle classes of the late 1960s and early 1970s. This was carried in a trailer towed behind Dad's Mark II Cortina over most of the South and South West of England during that period. Many of their visits to 'the Continent' were accompanied by her brother Ernest and his family. His first visits to that land mass had been made in uniform during the Second World War. He had seen active service throughout but, characteristically, rarely spoke about it.

In December 1990 I made a career change that raised my own standard of living considerably with immediate and long term effect but she died suddenly only six days later. Heavy snow had prevented me making a weekend visit and when Dad called to break the news to me in the early hours of a cold Monday morning there was still some road-clearing spadework to do before the funeral directors arrived to take charge.

The only benefit she derived from my improved position was her one and only use of a cell phone. A mere fourteen years after we had first had a land-line telephone installed in the house she sat on the plush leather seats of my new car, a Ford Sapphire 2000E, and made a call to Lucy; I drove away with that image and never saw her alive again.

She was a great admirer of Cousin Brian and the B.A. after his name. She was overwhelmed with pride when I achieved the same accolade. My B.A. is in Law and she was visibly disappointed when some years later I took the option of adopting the more explicit LL.B. instead.

The subsequent academic achievements of her grand children would have been beyond her wildest dreams.

Or would they? Another of her sayings was 'Always aim for the stars because you will always have the rooftops to land on if you miss'

She was sixty one years and seven months old precisely when she died and I shall not knowingly change my calendar in advance until I at least match that age.

Dot

Have not a blackened heart, my Son.
Change not the date till break of dawn.
No pedicure till Sabbath's done.
And red with white must not be worn.

Thomas á Becket was her key
to all that happened in the past.
'Fermez la porte' she said, with glee,
from Adams where her die was cast.

Such are the things my Mother said,
when I was young and keen to learn.
She also kept me clean and fed
my will to work and take my turn.

Then one cold night she left this life,
some thirty years too soon for me.
I lost the chance to ease the strife
that she'd endured continuously.

As if to lift my heavy load,
my fortunes rose, too late for Dot.
But all she said had made the road
for me to follow, from my cot.

As I approach her final age,
I wonder 'Shall I end the same?'
So words I set upon this page
act as letters after her name.

On September 12th 1953, Senator John Fitzgerald Kennedy married Jacqueline Bouvier in the United States of America. It was probably that event that prevented the World from reading that on the same day in Bartley Green, Denise Madeleine Cull was born. Family folklore has it that her forenames were those of her father's two favourite barmaids but Ernest Arthur Cull was also known to be a great admirer of the film star Madeline Carroll so, as far as I am concerned she was named after the actress, with the name 'Denise' being placed in front only because 'Madeleine' would have seemed pretentious in post-war working class Birmingham. They would not have been aware at that time that Miss Carroll was born only about five miles away in West Bromwich and that Madeleine was also her middle name, her first name being 'Edith'.

In 1994, Denise became Mrs Woodall but had been a constant source of support and encouragement for my various endeavours for several years before then. Those endeavours of course include my work for the old school association of which preserving the memory of Madeleine Carroll was part, as I went to the same school as she did, albeit a couple of generations later.

So, when I wrote my 'Sonnet to an Old Throstle' in honour of the older Madeleine, it became necessary for me to write one for the younger Madeleine too. Young Madeleine, or Denise if you insist, was known as 'Denny' until I inadvertently changed it to 'Deni' the first time I wrote it down. I am no Professor Higgins nor does she need one; she is an innately generous and caring person who gives freely of her time and money to those who need it but, like me, draws a line at scroungers and wastrels. This includes those who manipulate the 'nanny society' by taking out more than they need and certainly far more than they put in.

She is in many ways like the mother-in-law that she hardly had time to get to know but whom she replaced in providing some measure of steadying influence on my reckless and outspoken ways.

Unlike Dot, she was able to achieve the potential of her intellect by gaining a very good honours degree in Law despite a variety of domestic difficulties and concerns about her own health which are always present. 'The Class Act of '53' is my small tribute to an amazing lady.

The Class Act of '53

There is a lady, as fair as any
that Pygmalion himself could create.
To most of us she is known as Deni -
wife, daughter, step-mum, sister, aunt or mate.

Kind of heart, she would give her last penny
to those who need help to postpone their fate.
Charity cases, although so many
deserve more funding to come from the State.

To give them aid of course she would borrow,
but not for those who would take it by stealth.
Her life has been touched by pain and sorrow,
bereavement, worry and fear for her health.

But through it all, she looks to tomorrow
and cares for others, their love is her wealth.

I have already made the reader very well aware that I have a second cousin called Tina, of whose existence I have always known but whom I have only actually had within my circle of close friends and family for about two years. She is Christina Louise Negus (nee Batty) daughter of Margaret Batty (nee Woodall) and, like me, a great grandchild of Walter and Louisa (nee Slater) Woodall, a couple who feature in the poems that follow, along with several other family members including Tina's grandfather, Walter, and his younger brother Harold, who was my own grandfather. Old Walter's mother was Christiana (nee Halliday) and whether intentionally or not, Tina therefore carries something very close to the names of two of our shared forebears. Old Walter died just before I was born and I understand that Tina's memory of him is very vague. My memory of Louisa is equally vague, as I was very young when we met in Derby on no more than half a dozen occasions. Tina, on the other hand, remembers her well but mainly as a kindly widow still wearing mourning clothes for Walter. She was a Derby girl and carried the accent to prove it. I have many photographs of Louisa, one of which includes her son Harold, his son Dennis, and his son, me. Another photograph includes Tina and Robert who were close contemporaries but a generation apart. Walter and Louisa had five children who survived to enjoy reasonably full lives and one, Evlyna, who died in childhood. Walter (the younger) married two ladies called Margaret and had a daughter, also called Margaret, by the first; she became Tina's mother. Harold married May Leddington who gave birth to my father Dennis. Francis, always known by his middle name Leslie, married Hilda but had no issue. Alfred married Ethel (nee Stevenson) and had Brian and, eventually, Eva married William Birch and had Robert.

Despite being spectacularly attractive, or perhaps because of that, Eva's marriage came late in life and Robert was therefore only a few weeks older than Tina. 'Family Photographs' and 'Pennies on the Line' tell us a great deal about Robert, who never married and who died tragically at the age of thirty. He and I were born consecutively in the Woodall male line, separated only by Tina and her sister Gillian overall, but the ten year gap between us meant that I only knew him on roughly equal terms for a few years.

It may have been in 1964 at the funeral of Alfred but it was more likely in 1966 at the funeral of Walter that my involvement with the Derby Woodalls as a near adult began.

By 1972 Robert was also dead but that gave me time to learn that he and I were not exactly soul-mates. It was chilling in 2005 to be shown a photograph of him circa 1949 in which he was wearing clothes that I wore circa 1959 as his ever-thrifty mother handed them down to me as he grew out of them. I was at his funeral and can bear testimony to the images that Tina creates at the end of 'Family Photographs'. It was cold winter's day and the crematorium smoke did rise into a sky laden with incipient snowfall. Before we left Derby that day, Harold asked Dad and I to take him for a walk from Crewe Street, where Eva lived, to an area not far away called 'the Cavendish'. He stood and stared for a few minutes without speaking and then we left. When I arrived home from college the following evening I was met at the front door by Dad who told me that my dear 'Grandad' had died. He was 17 days short of his 77th birthday, had never fully retired and had cycled home to a cooked lunch, as he had done for more than 50 years, then died in his chair. Eva lasted another year and Leslie until 1975 when that generation came to a close. However, I have recently discovered that they had a cousin, Irene, who strongly features Eva at all earlier stages of life and who, at the time of writing, is a healthy 98 year old. I hope very much to meet her soon as surely it will be my last chance to embrace a grandchild of William and Christiana.

'Little Walter's Poem' is my own self-explanatory title for a piece held in the family archives kept by Brian. Unless Tina's grandfather was so advanced as to be able to compose a work about himself and Harold, this was written by their father in 1897. 'Dear Eva' is a letter written by Walter in verse to his daughter Eva whilst she was on holiday with her friend Lou Walker in 1939, a matter of weeks before the outbreak of World War II. The original hand-written copy is also held by Brian who at the age of four is the 'little man' referred to in the poem, he was staying with his grand-parents at the time. At different times, Brian, Tina and I have each been very fond of Eva and although with the best will in the World this work of her father cannot be classed as good poetry it is a lovely momento to have and is quite fittingly included in this book to sit alongside the offerings of several of his descendants. The few that follow include more by Tina, about our great grandmother and about Eva's son, Robert. There are also the two oldest poems in the book to which I referred at the start. 'Autumn', which is another poem written by Brian as a teenager is also included.

Great Grandmother

Come here, me duck,
Come stand by me and bring your story book.
I'll read to you, me duck,
Not Little Black Sambo again?
Eeh, she knows every word, you know,
I canna turn two pages together
Or it's, no, you've missed a bit,
Don't you, me duck.
Come on, then, I dinna mind.

Since the death of her husband,
She wore only black,
With perhaps a grey cardy, for a change.
She sat in her favourite chair,
Rock, rock, as hypnotic as the ticking of the clock,
As regular as breathing.
I stood by her black-skirted knee,
Enfolded by her black-sleeved arm,
Head against her black-garbed bosom,
Whilst she peered, weakly eyed at the page.

She sat, hours on end, whiling away the time,
Hands clasped, twiddling her thumbs,
First one way, now slowly, now quicker,
Then reversed, round and round,
As endlessly as the motion of the chair.
Why? I'd ask, Why do you do that?
I don't know, me duck, it's summat to do,
Keeps me company, when you're not here.

To my great-aunt she was Mam;
Mammam to my Mum.
To me she was stability itself,
Symbol of enduring, unconditional love:
My great grandmother.

Tina Negus

Family Photographs.

We were babies together at opposite ends of the huge black pram,
Sex-less in matching nighties. His mother, my mother's aunt,
Came late to marriage, with time to produce only one son.
As toddler's, hand-in-hand amongst the daisies, he smiled fearlessly
At the camera, neat in little shirt and shorts, my significant other.
Bobby Shafto, said his father fondly, ruffling his curls.
I smiled shyly, in white sunbonnet and hand-smocked dress.
I will marry you, he told me, when we're older.
At four, or five, relationships are vague; the grown-ups argued endlessly
About whether we were cousins once removed or second cousins,
But in any case it is only firsts, who are ill advised to marry.
I wondered if I would have any say in this arrangement.
Later, he turned sulky, the proposal used threateningly,
To be withdrawn if he could not bat first,
Or I refused to find the ball, or he lost at Monopoly,
Sending board and pieces crashing to the kitchen floor.
He would not look towards the photographer;
His father's hand hovered, directing his gaze,
In the background, the little tricycle, and the Noah's Ark.
On visits, we still shared a bed, though parental doubts grew ever stronger:
Apparent innocence, or at least naivety, persuaded.
We retired with paper, pencils, for night-time games: Hangman, Battleships,
Endless alphabetical lists of flowers, countries, rivers, body parts...
Provoking mutual investigation: we both were unimpressed.
Later he grew lanky, solitary, began photography himself;
His lengthy compositions producing frowns for all to see.
We drifted apart, me and my intended. He was withdrawn,
Tangled in a Gordian knot of undeveloped film,
Of confused thoughts and loneliness.
Family portraits ceased; he preferred railway scenes and locomotives.
Ironically, he died, falling, or jumping, from the train.
The black smoke from his winter burning, mingled
With the swirling white of driving sleet. His uncle perished the following day, chilled, they said, unto death,
Leaving me, to take the family photographs.

Tina Negus

Little Walter's Poem

I'm but a very little boy
And only just turned five
To help my mamma all I can
I every day contrive
I do a many little things
And play with brother too
We laugh and skip and jump and run
As all good children do
When it is dark we rest a while
With faces clean and bright
Prepare for bed then say our prayers
And kiss Mamma Goodnight.

Walter Woodall

This was written circa 1897 as if by Walter Woodall (but presumably with a good measure of help from his father, also Walter) with reference to his mother, Louisa, and his brother Harold who was born in 1895.

It is interesting to note that Louisa is referred to as Mamma at this time whereas all currently living members of the family remember her as Mammam. I wonder when and how the pet name changed.

Forty odd years later, the two little boys had been joined by other siblings and had all grown up. One of these, Eva, was enjoying a holiday with her friend Lou Walker which was certainly to be her last before the Second World War and perhaps her last before marriage and a small family of her own.

We don't know where she was staying but it seems that she wrote to her father either teasing or criticising him for an earlier effort: perhaps there were many poems of this type composed during that period. If so, only these two have survived.

Dear Eva,

I thank you for the picture card,
Its motto true to life
It is a devil of a job
To eat peas with a knife.

Of one small word I made a note
What was it? Let me see
I think it was something like this –
P - R - O - S - E.

I looked in my Reference Book
To see what that word meant
And found that "dull, uninteresting"
Was what I must have sent.

If this short note should prove the same
(For a poet I'll never be)
Just scan its message through, and then
Please drop it in the sea.

Our little man just counts the days
When you'll be here again
And then at night, when off to roost
"Another day gone" is his refrain

And in the morn we hear him say
"Why did Aunt Eva go away ?
Will she soon be back again?
Will she come back on Saturday?"

What will Aunt Eva bring me back
When she's done her holiday?
Will she bring some more tickets
That I with them can play?"

But now I'll stop, and wish you luck
For I'm no preacher and no talker,
Hoping the change will do you good
Both you and comrade, Miss Loo Walker. **Pop**

Train-spotting.

From the asphalt playground at the school, the main line, embanked
Between the station and the railway arch, formed the limit or our eastern view.
Inevitable, then, that a fascination with this last flowering of the age of steam
Should have occupied my childhood hours.
Penny platform tickets allowed access to a different world
Of timetables, and turntables, the taking in of water at the
Halfway point of the journey north or south,
And the changing of engines on a long haul;
A world of wheels and couplings, pistons, fire and smoke.

My cousin's rivalry gave added interest to the endless game
Of collecting numbers and engine names,
Still as clear in my memory today as in the lists we made nearly half a century ago.
The signal arm jerked and clanked warning of the next arrival;
Someone shouted "Peg's up!"
And the platform swarmed with small boys clutching dog-eared books
And pencil stubs, in expectation of a passenger express:
"The Flying Scotsman", "White Rose" Or "Norseman", bound
For Edinburgh, London, Leeds, or York.

The announcement crackled through the Tannoy system:
"Stand clear on Platform Three!"
As excited children shoved and jostled too near the edge.
Then the rumble on the rails swelled into a thunderous roar,
As a mighty Pacific giant flashed past, sparks flying from the glowing fire,
In a buffeting gale of strength and power; "Woodcock", "Gannet", "Falcon",
"Wild Swan", and often "Mallard", the speed record breaker.
Some we tired of, used to their daily passing,
But "Mallard" commanded constant respect, greeted with cheers or silent awe.

Once, the great “Sir Nigel Gresley”, long signalled, long awaited,
Crept past the platform, walking pace, with a heavy trail of wagons carrying ore.
Jeers of derision greeted this sad sight, as though a racehorse pulled a totter's cart.
Sheltering from the wind and rain in the up-line waiting room,
The lads inscribed their successes on the cream and green of railway paint;
“I copped Cock o’ the North”, or “Woolwinder” or “The Golden Fleece”.

Wheels slipping on the wet and greasy rails by the dripping water column,
The trains began their journey south,
Past the Roman High Dyke road, to the tunnel, and the summit of the line.

Gradually, my interest waned; my cousin no more kept track of numbers,
But occupied himself with photographs and sound effects;
Atmospheric reminders of this vanished time.
A bitter irony that I inherited his collection after his untimely death:

He fell,
Crashing from the carriage door, lay dead, upon the railway line.
His recordings I have kept unheard; the sounds of whistles,
Hissing steam, and the juddering of wheels,
Recall too uncomfortably the passing of the years and the innocence of children.

Runner-up in Partners 19th Open Competition, 2004.

Tina Negus

Graham.

And so I take up this pen,
his pen, inscribed with name, address and number of his phone,
and write these lines
to this man, whom I had never known,
till now.

Oh, I had heard of him,
can even now hear my mother say his name,
heard the affection in her voice
when she spoke of his father,
her little fair-haired cousin.
But he was but a name,
till now,
positioned on the family tree,
with no reality.

He was not flesh and blood,
till now:
remained an unrealised twinkle in his father's eye.
Indeed his Dad remained for me
forever fixed with golden infant curls,
a darling boy to bring forth love:
a playmate for the girls,
and for my doting mum.

And yet, unseen, unknown, this man has grown,
has wife and children of his own,
and is a friend to me.
This man,
who I had never known, till now.

For Graham and Dennis with love.

Tina Negus

Autumn

As always obeying Nature's rule
Summer heat begins to cool
Winds get colder, blowing hard
Husks of wheat round farmers' yard
All day long, an endless patter
As russet leaves begin to scatter
Early frosts do give alarm
When one sees the pool, calm
And lightly frozen, splinter;
This is a sign of oncoming winter
Fogs and mists are Autumn's ally
Soon they swirl and all things die
And choke under a clammy shroud
Everything engulfed in a dark, dank cloud

Brian H. Woodall c.1953

War

It should already be clear that, in my opinion, Wilfred Owen was one of the greatest poets that ever lived. I certainly regard two of his poems to be in the top three of the best poems ever written although I have changed my mind from time to time as to which one of the three is best. The trio is completed by a poem which must stand alongside Wordsworth's 'Daffodils' as the one most frequently forced upon school children during much of the twentieth century. I refer of course to 'If' by Rudyard Kipling. No prizes for guessing that the two from Owen are 'Anthem for Doomed Youth' and one that I have already mentioned by way of an excuse for giving pretentious Latin titles to poems that will never be hailed as classics; I mean of course 'Dulce et Decorum Est'.

The line 'Across my world a shadow once was cast' came to me sometime in the middle to late 1960s, probably in 1968. It was inspired by a poem written by my close friend at the time, Lisbeth Brown, which was itself inspired by a film we saw together called 'On the Beach' based upon a novel by Nevil Shute. Like most of our contemporaries, she and I, possibly out of conviction but more likely because it was fashionable, were strongly anti-war. Not being American and therefore having no direct right to speak about Vietnam, we focused our protests on the concept of a nuclear World War. Lisbeth's poem started thus:-

The watery sun cast shadows on my bed
as I awoke, sat up, looked round and said
'I'm glad I'm alive'

It continued for several stanzas using the same last line and then with the final one ending 'I wish I were dead'.

I once set this poem to music but by then the commercial appeal of protest songs had been exhausted by the likes of Dylan, Donovan, Baez, McGuire and even Buffy St.Marie so I didn't have to address the matter of shared royalties! I never did write the poem that I had intended to write but, instead, I eventually used the line to start one of my WW1 poems and, in deference to its age, I used part of it as the title of this book. The title of my poem is either another tribute to Owen or simply my way of saying that there is nothing 'great' about war. You can easily work out the rest of it for yourself.

Bellum Magnum Non Erat Bonum

Across my world a shadow once was cast
by The Great War, its name for twenty years.
As "Great" as Fire of London in the past
but worse than that, the cause of far more tears.
So why, when blades of mine were never honed
nor did I take the shrapnel and the gas,
am I compelled to speak in angry tones
of those four years that took so long to pass?
It's not because my brother fell in France
nor did my mother suffer widowhood.
And social change gave me a better chance
to rise than early bearers of my blood.
The reason for my wrath is simply said -
I mourn the countless rows of needless dead.

My various visits to Austria have already been mentioned, or at least some of them have - the skiing trips of my youth having been sidelined for now because of the paucity of poetry that came from them. During the same visit that spawned 'Salzkammergut', Denise and I took a bus to Bad Ischl one day, with mixed results. My grasp of the language proved to be insufficient to convince a pharmacist that there is in existence an effective remedy for heartburn without recourse to herbal preparations. On the positive side, we bumped into our friend, Rex Burton, with whom we shared coffee, cake and conversation for an hour or so. We also visited the Kaiservilla, the summer home of Emperor Franz Josef and his wife Elizabeth about whom more can be read later. Guided tours of the Kaiservilla were conducted regularly and the language used by the respective guides tended to be dictated by the nationality of the paying guests. It was clear that there was little demand for English and, although we are comfortable in German speaking restaurants and the like, a much wider vocabulary is needed for situations like that. We therefore took a guide sheet printed in English and did an unaccompanied tour between two German speaking parties. At one point, the party ahead had moved from the Emperor's study through one door at the precise moment that we had entered it through another. We were alone in the room in which the declaration that acted as the whistle to start World War I was written. I could not resist breaking the house rules to sit in a leather chair that still bears the maccassa oil stains absorbed from the head of Franz Josef during his habitual afternoon naps. The remainder of the tour of the house was perhaps less dramatic but certainly at least as revealing. I have no doubt that his pastimes were regarded as normal and acceptable at the time for a man of his rank, but this house proudly displayed the skulls of hundreds of chamois, numbered and dated, with the 2000th victim having been stuffed and mounted in whole!

Franz Josef had come to the throne as a very young man and had soon gained a very beautiful and even younger wife. He was already an old man when he found himself in a position from which his only realistically possible course of action can now be seen to have led to the first major conflict of the twentieth century. His wife and son had both died in tragic circumstances, and when his nephew and heir, Franz Ferdinand, took the bullet of the Serbian, Gavrillo Princip, in Sarajevo, he must have felt that the end, which for him actually came two years later, had already arrived.

A Chair at Kaiservilla, Bad Ischl

I sat upon a peaceful leather chair.
For sixty years Franz Josef did the same
then rose, with war on Serbia to declare
but was it more than just another game?
He'd shot two thousand chamois, just for sport,
and countless other beasts and birds as well.
The Serbs had shot his nephew so he thought
that millions more should fall the way **he** fell.

He'd upset Russia when the chair was new
but had not made new Allies at that time.
His wife was dead and friends of his were few,
his own life was no longer at its prime.
Two years he saw, his heir another two
by when his world was mainly blood and lime.

There was a time when I thought that all the First World War poetry that was needed to be written had already been written and, more importantly, it had been written by participants in the conflict, though not necessarily active combatants. A.E.Housman, Rudyard Kipling, Jessie Pope and Vera Brittain are some of the names that spring to mind as non-fighters, for differing reasons but principally because they were too old or of the wrong gender. In the unlikely event that Shirley Williams ever reads this, I do hope that she will forgive me for including her brilliant mother's name in the same sentence as that of the rather silly Jessie Pope. There is no comparison between either the war effort or the literary skills of those two ladies.

I later realised that millions of people, including me, know far more about that war than most of the poets associated with it could possibly have known. The incomparable Wilfred Owen, for example, never even knew the outcome of it nor any of its eventual consequences. He died in battle precisely one week before the Armistice and the church bells were ringing for victory and peace at the moment that his parents were given the news of his death. After this realisation I felt more comfortable and indeed more entitled to write on the subject but until then I had felt like an intruder: a cuckoo in the nest of a species that had been endangered for a century and which was now more or less extinct.

Nevertheless, the urge to write about 'The Great War' was irresistible and one of the products that emerged as a compromise was 'Pity'. Yet again, the title came from Owen as did the first line. It is in effect a summary of a dozen or so of the best known poems of World War I, written by some of the best known poets. Allusions to these men and to their work form the backbone of the poem but, I hope, I have given it a spin where necessary to underline my own views.

I did write notes clarifying these allusions but I have decided not to include these here. Rather, I have taken the view that any reader sufficiently interested in the subject will either recognise them immediately or will derive some pleasure from having to think more deeply or even to indulge in a little research. To those, beware! There is one allusion to an earlier conflict as well as to writings that have nothing whatsoever to do with war but they do have relevance.

PITY

"All the poet can do is to warn"
said the boy from Salop, and he did.
Freed from Hell a week before the Dawn
of a world without war, they had said.

But a false dawn it was, not a doubt
had his friend with the Military Cross
who, in shock, had taught the boy to shout
of the madness, the killing, the loss.

A Cross for himself came to the boy,
for his bravery when back in the field,
made to sound more like a place of joy
than the bloodbath that flooded that weald
by one more doomed lad, who thought it grand,
and the doctor who died before Dawn.

It's poppies, they said, that grow in the land
that's part of England, but many still mourn.

The soldier who sniffed that saffron smoke,
and was felled by the famed guns of Loos,
knew that death was the end, the final stroke
given easy by those that can choose.

Mouthless, faceless, lifeless – blind to tears
are the dead and so shall they remain.
This boy saw much, in less than two years,
claiming inches of useless terrain.

A poor Jewish boy, and one weak in mind
were united in age and in thought
of the shame of a war of this awful kind,
men trenched with rats or on wire caught.

Those red wet things and verminous shirts
were visions that would trouble the sane.
So what fools were they who ordered such hurt?
Could they picture or suffer such pain?

Throughout it all, reading Latin and Greek,
the Professor at Cantab had stayed.
He lauded Ypres and shillings per week
but his lancer was differently paid.

A true Shropshire lad gave the bare facts,
a lie written in Latin exposed –
millions lost to meaningless pacts
whilst those men who had signed them reposed.

When introducing 'Summer of Love' I referred to a second poem that had been inspired by a single incident occurring in 1967 and which lasted no more than five minutes from start to finish. The odd thing is that there was a gap of at least a decade between the final revision of the first poem and the germ of an idea for the second. From the date of the incident giving rise to the first poem until the publication of the second the gap is just about four decades.

I refer of course to 'The Old Soldier' which, I believe, needs little if any further introduction. It is certainly a sonnet, probably a Shakespearean sonnet, and has no hidden meanings whatsoever. However, it has a synergy with 'Summer of Love': a chance meeting of two people living geographically close to each other but having been born half a century apart.

To some extent, and certainly at different times, the fortunes of each were influenced by the other but not by equal amounts. At the time of the brief encounter it was taking me precisely forty eight minutes to earn two shillings as a part-time green grocer's assistant and the only things I had to spend it on were self-indulgent recreational items such as beer, cigarettes and gramophone records; I bought Beatles' singles as soon as they were released and Beatles' albums (LPs as we called them in those days) as soon as I could raise the money

I have no idea whether or not the other party spent a single day on the Somme, or four years entrenched there or nearby, or whether his injury and incapacity had come from an entirely different source. He may have been a total reprobate who got hurt performing some illicit act and whose obvious breathing difficulties stemmed from a lifetime of cigarette smoking.

My gift to him was very small indeed if his to me had been to endure a lifetime of suffering as a result of a genuine desire to give my generation a better life. However, if he had given himself a serious illness by a habit funded by, figuratively speaking, eventually getting his hand caught in the till, then I was the more generous.

I know which version I prefer to believe and for it I thank you, Old Soldier!

The Old Soldier

"You're in the Staffords now," the Sergeant said,
a shilling placed within the young man's hands.
And **too** young, by the way, but he'd been led
to list for King and Country by the band.
At eighteen almost all of him came back
with liquid lungs and half an arm blown off
by German lads with orders to attack.
His sweetheart couldn't bear to hear his cough.

For fifty years, he's trudged the park alone
as work and love have rarely passed his way.
Although the sunshine warms his aching bones
the sadness in his heart won't go away.
A kind young man puts two bob in his hand:
perhaps it **was** worthwhile to make that stand.

I think that I have always known the name 'Victor Silvester'.

He was a dance band leader serving a generation before my own interests in such mating rituals commenced. By my time, the beat was being provided by the likes of Chris Farlowe and the Thunderbirds at the West Bromwich Adelphi, embryonic stars such as the Move and the Moody Blues at the Handsworth Plaza and icons like the Beatles at Birmingham Odeon which, in December 1965, were the headline act of the first pop concert that I attended. Both dancing, even in the aisles, and listening to the music were prevented by the hysterical behaviour of hundreds of adolescent girls, screaming like the Sabine women should have screamed, whilst pledging themselves to one or all of the Fab Four.

Dances like the Twist and the Shake did not rely upon the roll-out mat showing foot positions that the Quickstep and the Foxtrot required. To the indignation of my dad, one of my girlfriends once referred to those as 'Old Time Dances', a genre which for him meant those dances that included the Polka and the Gay Gordons.

I cannot recall how it came about, nor when, but many years after I had last heard his name mentioned in any context, I learned that Victor Silvester, who was named in celebration of the victorious outcome of the Boer War so I am given to understand, was a boy soldier in World War I and before he was actually old enough to enrol, other than by lying about his age, he had been put on several firing squads to dispatch fellow soldiers accused of cowardice in the field.

In his autobiography, entitled 'Dancing is my life', he rccalls a particular execution, the first in which he participated, in some detail and this is the basis of my poem.

In my research I of course learned that his story has been challenged for its truth and that some have put forward convincing cases to the effect that his army career lasted only as long as it took his mother to track him down and bring him home.

I did write a sixth verse to 'Silvester' which started with the line:-
'Lies, lies, nowt but lies'
but I scrapped it within days of writing – I never could see a good reason to allow facts to get in the way of a good story!

SILVESTER

"Left.... Left..... Left, Right, Left"
the subaltern barked as the squad marched out.
The dawn sun shone through a cleft
in the cloud that shrouded this latest bout
of death dealt by those bereft
of care, compassion, common sense or doubt.

Guns were raised, orders given,
trigger fingers twitched on trembling hands.
Shots rang out, loud and even,
to send a scared boy to the promised land.
Alive, praying for heaven,
the boy dragged his chair across wet, red sand.

But the subaltern caught him
in two quick strides. Then one close range bullet
and the weak dawn light grew dim.
Now with blood or tears all eyes were full, it
made them weak in heart and limb
and their breakfast to rise in the gullet.

One squad lad had served three years
but he was just seventeen at the time.
Four times more he, with his peers,
had to play in this evil pantomime.
Sent home hurt, Mum in tears,
playing truant to sign up was **his** crime.

"Slow....Slow.... Quick, Quick, Slow"
His new dancing beat was known to them all
in the Palais de Danse so
the Theatre of War turned into a ball.
Light of foot, he beat the foe
and his name is not on Thiepval's wall

There are many songs that I wish I had written, lyrics, music or both. Most genres are covered by that wish – Classics, Operatic, Rock, Popular and Folk to name but a few. There are many goals that I wish I had scored, David Beckham's for England against Greece in 2001 probably heading that particularly long list, with Jeff Astle's against Everton at Wembley in the 1968 F.A. Cup Final running it a close second. David Platt's against Belgium in the 1990 World Cup is also in the running. The set of six scored by George Best against Northampton in a cup game immediately upon his return from a 28 day suspension was to die for and I always find it amusing, when I see the recording of that game, that my friend and former WBA defender, Ray Fairfax, who was marking George that day, can be seen in the frame for only one of those goals and then for less than 1 second! Many years later, the Sunday newspapers carried a picture of Michael Owen about to score his fourth for Liverpool in a 6 nil thrashing of the Baggies. Many individuals in the crowd including my son Andrew, who was coached in his younger days by Ray Fairfax, could be seen in the picture but not a single Baggies' defender! There are many people from all eras that I wish I had met – Jesus of Nazareth, Saint Ralph Sherwin, Isaac Newton, Isambard Kingdom Brunel, Prince Albert, Winston Churchill, Madeleine Carroll, John Lennon and Margaret Thatcher for examples, and each for entirely different reasons.

Needless to say, there are also many poems that I wish I had written, most of these having been referred to elsewhere in this book. However, there is one in particular that, in this category, stands above all others and I have neither referred nor alluded to it earlier but I include it here in full for you, dear reader, to savour and I have no doubt to admire as much as I do. Its author is none other than my darling wife Denise whose talents have never ceased to astonish me. I am so full of admiration for her as a professional and as an academic that I am sometimes guilty of overlooking the fact that she is a wonderful wife and one hell of a sexy lady!

But I digress. 'I can't stop thinking' is all hers. It needs no explanation nor any further introduction. Privately, I love the concept of an intelligent twenty first century woman putting Jessie Pope and her ilk in their place. White feathers indeed! What say you to that, my lady?

This poem is brilliant, evocative, simple but all-embracing and, above all, it could only have been written by one person, my Deni.

I can't stop thinking.........

I can't stop thinking about the men in the trenches,
the lice, the vermin, the barbed wire fences.
They should be home canoodling with wenches.
I can't stop thinking about the men in the trenches

I can't stop thinking about the boys on The Somme,
Ypres or Mons, they all merge into one.
Millions of mothers losing their son.
I can't stop thinking about the boys on The Somme.

I can't stop thinking about the sweethearts and wives
left at home, as they were, to get on with their lives.
The horror of war their future deprives.
I can't stop thinking about the sweethearts and wives

I can't stop thinking about those who were shot.
Not by the enemy but by those who had not
the compassion to recognise these poor wretches' lot
I can't stop thinking about those who were shot.

I can't stop thinking that war is not right.
Far better to talk than to take up the fight.
Ignore the misguided with their feathers of white.
I can't stop thinking that war is not right.

I can't stop thinking.................

Denise M. Woodall

As with 'Pity' I have written explanatory notes for 'Isandlwana' but I do not reproduce them here in full.

I first saw the film 'Zulu' soon after it was released in 1964 and I would estimate that I have watched it on average once every three years since then, including once with sub-titles one rainy day on holiday somewhere in mainland Europe.

'Isandlwana' has more in common with the later and less well known film, 'Zulu Dawn' to the extent that it only mentions the Rorke's Drift affair in passing. Whilst this remarkable event, comparable in many ways to the Dunkirk retreat sixty years later, was both commendable and indeed well commended, it was a useful tool with which those responsible for the embarrassing reversals elsewhere could deflect censure.

Frere and Chelmsford were the two principals in the pantomime that was the battle of Isandlwana. Although Frere's guilt is the greater for the simple reason that his actions were the main cause of the Zulu wars, Chelmsford's inept handling of his forces in the field, the effect in no way mitigated by the actions of some of his lieutenants, was the more proximate cause of heavy losses.

It is very sad to reflect that few lessons had been learned by the British Army thirty five years later when faced in the field of conflict by a much more equally armed opponent.

It is one of life's ironies that almost all of the leading players in this particular Act from the full British War Drama died either young, disgraced or both. The exception was Lord Chelmsford who lived long enough to see the Boer War and the accession to the throne of Edward VII before dying at a ripe old age whilst playing billiards in his London club.

As a poem, it needs several readings for familiarisation but after that I hope you like the form and rhythm of it.

ISANDLWANA

Bring Boer, Black and British folk under one rule
was the task set for Sir Bartle Frere.
Forty thousand Zulus, an army in fact,
did not wish to yield nor to sign such a pact.
"Without a war" had said London, worried elsewhere,
but the Consul knew no other tool.

Cetshwayo was told to disband or else
the might of the Empire he would feel.
No concession like that could be made, Bartle knew,
as the British were trained but relatively few.
So Lord Chelmsford, who before his Empress would kneel,
invaded, as Trollope later tells.

At one mile per day they reached Isandlwana Hill
and established base camp for the fray.
Two thirds of the force was sent off south east
but north east and close were twenty thousand at least.
They were spotted by scouts so attacked the same day.
The camp fought back but chances were nil.

Warnings went out but by Chelmsford dismissed
then news of the attack was relayed
to Colonel Harness who sent a relief squad back
but was stopped by the Peer who denied the attack.
At the camp, fierce fighting meant the full price was paid
by hundreds of men, now on a list.

Izimpondo zankomo is how they describe
the shape of the attack by the horde.
The horns of the buffalo contain the defence
whilst pressure is applied by the head, much more dense.
With twelve men to one into the base camp they poured,
spears won the day - but guns halved the tribe.

A gross of good soldiers was grudgingly led
to defend Rorke's Drift from attack.
Chard and Bromhead were equals in both station and rank
but the lower class Dalton is whom they must thank.
He inspired the men to force the horde back
again and again, as the soil turned red.

Not a victory as such, just a solid defence
but to Chelmsford it provided support.
In his swift note to London he reported this ace,
over King Cetshwayo, to avoid the disgrace.
Chard and Bromhead's loyal silence with medals was bought;
Dalton's VC was to stay future tense.

Politicians and press were united at home
in demands for Lord Chelmsford's recall.
Lord Beaconsfield was alone in resisting this cry,
to avoid the Queen's wrath he joined in with the lie.
Dead Durnford was damned for Isandlwana's fall;
and shortage of shot for the tombs.

Weakened by illness and by political swing
the Prime Minister altered his stance.
Chelmsford was replaced under African skies
then to Victoria at home he dealt a pack of lies.
She showered him with honours as if in his trance,
he was her hero and under her wing.

With Gladstone back in power and Beaconsfield dead,
Consul Frere was sacked and disgraced.
Cetshwayo was exiled, and Dalton died sad,
and the real Rorke's Drift heroes were only a fad.
Chelmsford lived longer but then died in a haste
at his club, with a cannon off red.

For any reader who has remained to this stage of the book I have got some great news – you are almost at the end! You will by now have formed some opinion of me and you will have identified some of my main interests in life. You will have found that although I have regarded Lichfield as my home for many years, I was born and raised in West Bromwich and that I still have very close ties with both its leading school and its football club. It will not have escaped your notice that I have travelled a good deal but that I have never been massively impressed with other parts of the World. It is also self-evident that I managed to avoid being brain-washed by the so-called comics of the 1950s in each of which some gung-ho sergeant or wing commander murdered a few dozen of their German or Japanese counterparts in every issue. As a child I was never comfortable with that type of jingoism and by the mid 1960s I had become very strongly anti-war. Fortunately, it was fashionable to think that way at the time but I was naturally very comfortable with the 'Make love not war' ideal. Nevertheless I loved Johnny Speight's line about us beating the Germans in two World Wars and one World Cup. Sadly, there never has been anything amusing about the Japanese. 'An die Gefallenen' grew out of two events within six months of each other and brings together several of the interests mentioned above.

In November 2005, the beautiful oak-clad pipe organ in my old school hall which had been built in remembrance of former pupils who died in World War I and which had panels added later to include victims of World War II, was officially registered as a War Memorial and a service of re-dedication was held. I had walked, pedalled or driven my Vespa the mile from my family home to the school many times during my years as a pupil there and it was a privilege to make the slightly longer journey that day.

In May 2006 I found myself in Saint Wolfgang's Church in Salzkammergut looking at another organ, this one being beautiful in its own way but surprising metallic in appearance. Close to it were the lists of local lads who died in the World Wars and two facts hit me right between the eyes. Perhaps obviously, boys of the same tender ages as our own fallen were mourned by our erstwhile enemy and, more significantly, the sons of some of the ones on the first list appeared on the second.

When will we ever learn?

An die Gefallenen

I know two organs, far apart
in distance and in style.
One by a lake in Osterreich
and one, from home, a mile.
The nearer one is cloaked with oak
the other gilded bright.
With finials and angels fair
to match that splendid site.

Two organs, so, two towns of course,
each one is home for some.
And both were home to others once,
before their time had come.
The wood belonged beside the lake,
the metal near the foundry.
Yet each town used the other's craft,
it seems taste knows no boundary.

Each organ has two lists nearby,
the names of those who fell.
Auer und Weis, Adams and Wood;
for those there was no bell.
The later lists are larger yet,
as lessons were not learned.
Auer and Wood are there again,
their fathers' murders spurned.

The Sisi Set

I must have been vaguely aware of the existence of Emperor Franz-Josef from the first time that I heard about the causes of the Great War. However, the first time that I recall having consciously registered him was in 1975 on a skiing trip to the small village of Nauders, near to Switzerland's St. Moritz but actually in Austria, and also very close to the Italian border.

In those pre-Euro days, his face seemed to be on every banknote, every postage stamp and on one in every five street names. Considering the fact that he had been dead for nearly sixty years by then, it seemed to me to be a remarkable memorial matched only, in that part of the World, by Mozart himself.

However, he had been over-shadowed in my mind by another Emperor, Kaiser Wilhelm II, to the extent that I had almost forgotten that the delightful Austrians had not only been batting for the other side in the Great War but that they had actually started it!

The intervention of World War II and the embarrassment of sharing a Nationality with Herr Hitler probably served to make the people I would meet deceptively pro-English. Poor old Franz-Josef had also been over-shadowed by his nephew and heir, Franz-Ferdinand, whose only contribution to history, apart from throwing a tantrum over whom he should marry, was to take Princip's bullet in Sarajevo.

At least one historian of my acquaintance attributes even that to a faulty gearbox on his Renault which prevented his driver engaging reverse gear at a time when retreat would have been a great move.

Nevertheless, Franz-Josef ruled his Empire for even longer than Queen Victoria ruled Britannia, and made relatively few mistakes. One of these was in falling out with the Russians early in his reign. This was not a bad move in itself but made much worse, eventually terminal, by failing to replace them as friends with any significantly powerful race. It did not occur to me for some considerable time that this guy was a serial runner-up and that he had already been upstaged by his loopy son who had entered a suicide pact with a very young girlfriend at their 'holiday home', Mayerling.

But, and this is where I come to the point, also by his beautiful, intelligent and accomplished wife.Elizabeth of Bavaria was, relatively speaking, of lesser aristocracy than Franz-Josef although they were cousins.

She was a World-class horsewoman whilst his sporting trophies comprise nothing more than the stuffed or otherwise preserved remains of thousands of helpless creatures. I am not talking about the victims of his war here, just the birds and animals he proudly shot, like fish in a barrel, on his estates.

The similarities between Elizabeth, known as Sisi, and Diana, Princess of Wales are astonishing: in some ways not unlike those between Abraham Lincoln and John Kennedy. Beautiful, dutiful and dynastically directed, maritally unhappy, narcissistically frustrated by age and gravity and, ultimately, the victim of a violent end shrouded with intrigue and perpetuated by conspiracy theories.

Sisi was evidently the more intelligent of these two unfortunate ladies and spent many of her lonely hours writing poetry in preference to whinging to any nineteenth century equivalent of Andrew Morton or Martin Bashir, although it seems that she did her fair share of cosying up to the Will Carlings and James Hewitts of the day! 'Bay' Middleton, later suggested by many as being the real father of Clementine Hosier, being an example

I have taken half a dozen of these poems and their literal translations into English and re-written them. It is quite beyond my linguistic abilities to make a serious attempt at true translations that would also retain the poetic form of the original German. I have therefore concentrated on the poetry rather than the grammar. My own resultant English versions have the same metres and rhyming patterns as Sisi's originals had and I have also attempted in places to both broaden and to modernise her work. The titles are mine.

From the handful of short poems that follow, the sadness of this bird in a gilded cage can be sensed. Imagine her with fading, film-star looks sitting alone in some of the most beautiful palaces and gardens on Earth, owned by her husband as head of one of the most powerful empires on Earth but for whom she appears to have had little affection.

It does have a familiar ring to it, I think.

Longing

Fresh Spring returns, splendid beyond words,
which trims the trees with new green hue
and teaches new songs to this year's birds
and makes the flowers glow with dew

But what can Springtime bliss be to me
here in this distant land so strange?
I long for the Sun of home, you see,
I long for that river's soft range.

The Path

Oh had I but never left the path
that would have led me to be free
Oh that on the broad way of this wrath
and pride I never came to be.

I have awakened in a prison
with golden chains which bind, I see.
But now my yearning always is on
freedom which turned away from me

I have awakened from a rapture
which did my youthful spirit stay.
And, vainly, do I curse that capture
in which I bet freedom away

Abandoned

In my great loneliness I dwell
and I make my songs alone
My heart with grief and sadness fills
and weighs my spirit down

Once I was so young and richly
blessed with love of life and hope.
Nothing matched my strength and keenly
with the open world I coped

I loved, I lived, and loved some more
as through the World I wandered
But never reached what I strove for
as truths were ever squandered.

Peace

Sweden, Oh life is better there,
we shall always envy you.
Across the sea without a care
the good folk are happy too.

Their rulers can admit with pride
that many lives have been saved.
True, armies do not there abide
and cannon strength has been waived.

Only in Bulgaria?

The poorest farm folk sweat,
working their fields of soil
in vain, for they never get
returns for all their toil.

Bullets, guns and bombs cost dear
with thousands used each day.
Especially with voting near,
to win the game their way.

Who knows, without our leaders
would there still be battles?
For costly war no need as
Victory's urge is settled.

Love and Wine

For me there is no love
nor wine for laughter.
They either give me pain
or sickness after.

Love can be sweet, but sour
and bitter it grows.
My wine is doctored but
helps me keep those vows.

Falser still than wine
often can be love.
We may pretend to kiss
but as thieves we move.

For me there is no love
nor wine for laughter.
They either give me pain
or sickness after.

www.ingramcontent.com/pod-product-compliance
Ingram Content Group UK Ltd.
Pitfield, Milton Keynes, MK11 3LW, UK
UKHW041939190726
13854UKWH00004B/1692

9 780955 677106